A GROUP OF ENGLISH ESSAYISTS

A GROUP OF

ENGLISH ESSAYISTS

OF THE

EARLY NINETEENTH CENTURY

BY

C. T. WINCHESTER

PROFESSOR OF ENGLISH LITERATURE
IN WESLEYAN UNIVERSITY

Essay Index Reprint Series

BOOKS FOR LIBRARIES PRESS, INC.
FREEPORT, NEW YORK

First published 1910
Reprinted 1967

PRINTED IN THE UNITED STATES OF AMERICA

To

OSCAR KUHNS

THE following papers pretend to no discovery of new biographical fact, nor to any reversals of established critical verdict. They are, for the most part, the result of many pleasant hours in a college seminary room; and their interest, if any interest they have, is that attending the informal discussion of a group of familiar and delightful English prose-writers.

If a disproportionate attention seems given in these pages to biography rather than to criticism, it should be remembered that Hazlitt, Lamb, De Quincey, Wilson, and Hunt all found their themes within their own personal experience. Perhaps no other body of English prose, equally large and important, is so exclusively autobiographical. The biographical method of approach, always useful, is here the only one open to the critic. He must first know the man before he can estimate the book.

CONTENTS

A GROUP OF ENGLISH ESSAYISTS

THE NEW ESSAY — JEFFREY AS CRITIC

I

VERY different literary forms have been designated by the common name Essay. In strictness, it is to Montaigne that we owe the name and the thing. His *Essais*, excellently translated by John Florio in 1583, were at once popular in England, and Bacon, fourteen years later, borrowed their title for his famous little bundles of apothegm. The influence of the *Essais*, continuing into the next century, increased with the liking for all things French after the Restoration, and is attested by Cotton's new translation in 1680. They evidently furnished the model for those charming discursive papers by Cowley, Halifax, and Temple, which closely resemble some of the best work of Hazlitt or Lamb.

But the sudden and immense popularity of the *Tatler* and *Spectator* in the Queen Anne time brought into prominence another type of the essay. It is the peculiar praise of Addison that he knew how to give permanent charm to the familiar, even to the trivial, by nicety of literary skill. His manner is simple, yet always easy and urbane. He had nothing of importance to say; but he could say it with a suavity, humor, and grace that make the veriest nothings admirable. He was no philosopher, no statesman, and a very mediocre critic, but his little papers on a fan or a petticoat, on the foibles of Sir Roger or the vanity of Ned Softly, may last as long as the *Paradise Lost,* and very probably find more readers.

For more than half a century, the acknowledged mastery of Addison tended to popularize this literary form in which he had won such success. Before the close of the century there had appeared more than a hundred periodicals, — most of them as short-lived as the flies of a summer, — which attempted to do what had been done so brilliantly in the *Tatler* and the *Spectator.* But they all failed. The ssay of the Addisonian type demands the skill of an Addison. It lost its distinctive charm even in the treatment of Goldsmith; and it becomes a solid, clumsy thing under the ponderous handling of Johnson in the *Rambler* and *Idler.* Before the close of the century its form was outgrown; the modern essay has a quite different origin.

For two hundred years, indeed, many excellent prose papers of moderate length, written upon weighty themes, political, philosophical, and critical, had appeared as prefaces, letters, pamphlets, and short treatises; but it was the new Reviews and Magazines, founded at the beginning of the nineteenth century, that produced the modern essay. Now, for the first time, we have that extended discussion of some one theme, popular in manner yet accurate in statement, and admitting high literary finish to which we now confine the name of essay. The founding of the *Edinburgh Review* in 1802, not only introduced to the public a new group of young liberal writers, it introduced a new type of writing, a type adapted to a wide range of subjects, giving expression to the author's personality, and affording scope for almost any kind of rhetorical excellence.

The *Edinburgh* had, indeed, been preceded by a number of so-called Reviews; [1] of which all but two were short-lived and of no influence. These two, however, the *Monthly Review*, founded in 1749, and the *Critical Review*, in 1756, were already of quite venerable age. Though they contained little but book-notices, for half a century they had been rival pretenders to the realm of English criticism. By looking over the correspondence of Fanny Burney

[1] The *London Review*, 1775–1780; *A New Review*, 1782–1786; the *English Review*, 1783–1796; the *Analytical Review*, 1788–1799.

or of Cowper, one may see how their verdicts were dreaded by young or timorous authors. The *Monthly Review* was conducted by that redoubtable Philistine, Ralph Griffiths, who starved and bullied Goldsmith, and furnished security for the poet's gay clothing at the price of four articles for the *Review*. Most of Griffiths' criticism, however, was written by feebler men, poor-devil authors whose opinions were always at his dictation. He paid them at the rate of two guineas a sheet of sixteen pages, and as their idea of a review was eight pages of quotation to one of criticism, they can hardly be said to have been underpaid. To the reader of to-day their writing seems so empty that we wonder how it could have been deemed a misfortune to be damned by such ignorant judges. On the appearance of Gray's *Elegy* the critic of the *Monthly* ventures only the opinion that "the excellence of this little poem may compensate for its lack of quantity." The Bentley edition, two years later, moved him to enthusiasm by the "head and tail pieces with which each poem is adorned, which are of uncommon excellence, the Melancholy in particular being exquisite." Occasionally, and especially toward the close of the century, a new author is greeted with something like intelligent recognition. The Kilmarnock edition of Burns, for example, by some rare good luck, was reviewed by some one able to discern, under the

Scottish dialect, — which he calls disgusting, — the genius of a new kind of poet. But, as a rule, it is difficult to discern any relation between the approval of the critic and the quality of the work. And there is seldom anything to break the deadly dulness of the writing save the rather spirited comments which each editor now and then bestows upon the other. For they were always at loggerheads. "The *Monthly Review*," said Griffiths, a year after the *Critical* was founded, "is *not* written by physicians without practice, authors without learning, men without decency, and gentlemen without manners." Smollett, editor of the *Critical*, rejoined with similar urbanity: "The *Critical Review* is not written by a parcel of obscure hirelings under the restraint of a bookseller and his wife. The writers for the *Critical* are unconnected with booksellers and unawed by old women."[1] Making allowance for editorial heat, each Review seems to have characterized the other not very unfairly.

With only these senile rivals in the field, the sudden and phenomenal success of the *Edinburgh Review* is no marvel. The familiar story of the meeting of those three eager but impecunious Edinburgh students, Sydney Smith, Brougham, and Jeffrey, when the *Edinburgh Review* was conceived, is a classic of literary history, and deserves to be. For the *Edin-*

---

[1] Forster's *Life of Goldsmith*, Book II, Ch. 1.

burgh was essentially a new thing. The idea seems to have been an unpremeditated suggestion of Sydney Smith's; there had been no happier literary inspiration since Richard Steele hit upon the plan of the *Tatler*, nor any more pregnant with results for our later prose literature. The three young enthusiasts were scholars and gentlemen, and they took their Review out of Grub Street at once. At first, indeed, it was proposed that the writers of articles should have no remuneration at all; that "it should be," as the biographer of Jeffrey puts it, "all gentleman and no pay." But this was thought to be a little too quixotic, and the wiser rule was adopted that all contributors should be required to take pay, and should be paid like gentlemen. The papers were to be much longer than those in the old Reviews; and, while they still retained the form of a review of a book or books, instead of being a mere list of quotations with a little commonplace comment, they were animated discussions of important subjects of contemporary interest, for which the books under notice served merely as a text. The writers evidently had opinions of their own: sometimes a little arrogant, sometimes a little shallow, but at all events not merely perfunctory; and they knew how to set forth those opinions with the spirit and the style of gentlemen. In literary matters the new Review was thought brilliant and magisterial; and in politics, at a time when conservatism was having everything its own way, these young men dared, if somewhat cautiously, to avow pronouncedly liberal opinions.

It is true that the reader of to-day who turns over the early volumes of the *Edinburgh* runs the risk of finding the luminary not quite so brilliant as the accounts of its reception have led him to expect. There is certainly not so much dash and audacity in the opening numbers as one would suppose from the surprise and indignation they excited. The writers seem rather to assume a dignified assurance of manner. But any one who prepares himself by a short course of reading in what called itself criticism before 1800 will find the most homiletical passages of the Review "stick fiery off indeed." And it must be remembered that there is not much duller reading to be found on earth than that between the covers of *any* Review a century old, with its pother over questions settled three generations ago, and over books and men alike gathered now to a forgotten past.

It is a more serious charge against these early volumes of the *Edinburgh* and of the *Quarterly Review*, established in 1807, that they contain little or nothing of permanent value as literature. Yet this, too, was inevitable. Perhaps the most important service of the two Reviews was the intelligent guidance of opinion on public affairs. By far the larger number of the articles were on such

7

subjects. But any periodical devoting its attention so largely to current political questions of the hour must be content to see most of its writing pass into that wallet wherein Time puts alms for oblivion. The article that is timely is seldom immortal. Only some unusual intensity, like Swift's, or some unusual philosophic vision like Burke's, can give to writing on such themes lasting value. And none of the early reviewers had either of these qualifications in any high degree.

For the literary criticism, which occupied considerable space in both Reviews, there is, perhaps, a little more to be said. The new Reviews doubtless did something to raise the quality of literary criticism. With their pretensions they could not afford to utter partial, hasty, ill-considered verdicts. Criticism was forced to justify its decisions, and to look about for some general principles. Doubtless nothing like a science of criticism was elaborated — it may be questioned whether there is any such a science; but the Reviews at least demanded from the critic careful reading, instructed judgment, and some definite views as to the grounds of literary excellence. They were, as has been said, a kind of college of criticism. Yet much of the resulting work was either very commonplace or very perverse. The Reviews certainly made some notorious mistakes. But critics, like the rest of us, are very fallible, and their worst mistakes might be pardoned them if it could be shown that they had often introduced to public notice genius not yet recognized, or removed unworthy prejudice, or anticipated in any way the verdict of the next generation. But that the Reviews rendered any such service, between 1800 and 1825, is very doubtful. A careful reading of all the critical notices in the *Edinburgh* and *Quarterly* during these years will prove that they usually followed the public taste, occasionally opposed it, but never led it. They echoed the popular admiration for Scott and Byron; but the other three great poets, Wordsworth, Shelley, and Keats, won recognition in spite of their neglect and abuse. Jeffrey's persistent attacks upon Wordsworth are matter of familiar knowledge, and unquestionably did something to retard the poet's fame; they set a fashion not yet quite outgrown. From 1815 to 1837 neither Review has anything to say of Wordsworth: having made up their verdict of condemnation, they refuse to alter or even to repeat it. Everybody remembers that the *Quarterly*, "so savage and tartarly," had the blame of killing John Keats; while the *Edinburgh* had no word of recognition for him, and only broke silence in 1820 when his brief career was closed. Shelley was abused by the *Quarterly* through three violent articles, and the cautious *Edinburgh* did not venture a word of him until 1824 — two years after he was dead.

Yet, after all, the most perverse literary criticism is not without value. It at least calls attention to the book. Probably the poet himself would rather be damned than ignored. And by the discussion of faults and merits, even by the opposition he provokes, the critic does something to educate public taste; the collision of opposite opinions generates a kind of literary atmosphere and not infrequently evolves something like critical principles. Had it not been for the blind dogmatism of the *Edinburgh*, we might never have had Coleridge's *Biographia Literaria*. The criticism of the last hundred years, begun by these Reviews, has certainly done much to render public interest in literature more general and more intelligent, and thus to raise the standard of production.

II

It must be admitted that in all this early critical writing there are but very few papers that will find a place among English classics. Southey furnished to the *Quarterly* a body of solid and sensible prose writing, mostly on political subjects, and all of it now dusty and dead. Gifford, the editor of the *Quarterly*, was a dull-sighted, thick-skinned, heavy-handed critic, with little acumen and no delicacy, who richly deserved the flogging he got from Hazlitt. He liked to pose as a literary judge and executioner, but he wrote comparatively little himself, and that little was never of much value. Of the *Edinburgh* men, Brougham, though a vigorous and careless writer, was never ambitious of literary repute. Sydney Smith was unsurpassed as a wit, raconteur, letter-writer; but his papers in the *Edinburgh* are mostly on ecclesiastical and political topics, and only two or three of them show him at his best. The critic among the reviewers was Francis Jeffrey. From 1802 to about 1830 he was accounted beyond question the first of literary critics. As the century advanced, his fame declined. His obstinate and contemptuous depreciation of Wordsworth was remembered against him when the poet had come to his own. There were a good many irreverent people of the later generation who thought his criticism, when not commonplace, merely smart. Yet as late as 1867 Carlyle pronounced him "by no means supreme in criticism or in anything else; but it is certain that no critic has appeared among us since worth naming beside him." And only the other day, in an able and discriminating study, Professor Gates [1] was protesting against the neglect of Jeffrey's good work in Jeffrey's own famous words "This will never do!"

It is easy to understand Jeffrey's contemporary popularity. In the first place, he wrote a clear, rapid, fluent English. Doubtless he is sometimes

[1] *Three Studies in Literature*, 1899.

too fluent and makes a little philosophy go a long way; but his style has a metallic brilliancy, not unlike that of his admirer, Macaulay. He knows how to say telling things, and he has infinite store of illustration. Then, too, like Macaulay, he is always cock-sure — which is pleasing in a critic. His sweeping assertions, his lavish use of the superlative and the unusual, give to his writing a magisterial air that most readers find very satisfying. Provided he agrees with us, — and Jeffrey never differed boldly with current opinion, — we like the critic to tell us authoritatively how we ought to feel about a book, and why we ought to feel so. We compliment ourselves on having reached substantially a sound judgment without his aid; and the loftier the critic, the greater the compliment of his agreement with us.

Then Jeffrey's criticism has always a certain hard common sense. It is clear and sane, level to the comprehension of everybody. There is nothing subtle in it. He never goes much below the surface, and cannot give you those penetrating glimpses that sometimes illuminate the whole of an author's work. He likes his meaning plain and his emotions familiar. Anything profound, mystical, or even strikingly original is likely to put him out. He emerges from the farther end of one of Wordsworth's long passages of transcendentalism blinking and angry. But the large, obvious excellences of thought and feeling, which all men perceive, he can state and appraise with intelligence and justice. He is best, therefore, on such objective writers as Scott; best of all, I think, on books like Mrs. Hutchinson's *Memoirs* or Pepys' *Diary*, that present no problems, and invite narrative treatment with copious illustrative quotations. But even in his most unsympathetic reviews, like those on the Lake School, his opinions, however blind, have a plausibility that recommends them to average prosaic common sense. He is never perverse or paradoxical of set purpose.

Jeffrey's method, unlike that of most recent critics, is dogmatic, never exactly what we have come to call impressionist. The modern critic strives to suggest the total effect upon himself of the work under review; to make you feel as the work has made him feel. He is the medium through which you are to be put *en rapport* with the author. Jeffrey's method is altogether different. He does not aim to give you an appreciation of the book, but an *estimate* of it. This is an intellectual process, a judicial process, the application of principles to reach a verdict. All Jeffrey's criticism is in this manner; he is always proving, expounding, defending. This method not only tends to conventional decisions, but it is unlikely to produce writing of the highest literary quality. For it does not appeal to our sympathy, but to our judgment; and it gives to the critic little room for the play of imagination or the expression of his own personality.

It is this method that determines the favorite form of Jeffrey's critical articles; for they are nearly all built on the same plan. They begin with an elaborate introduction, which often takes up about a third of the paper. This introduction is devoted either to a résumé of some period of literary history or to a statement of general principles on which his specific critical judgments are to be based; then follows, for the rest of the paper, a detailed estimate of the book, usually with copious excerpts to illustrate and enforce the verdict. These introductions, when of the historical sort, are usually correct in their facts, but they are superficial and show little sense of the deeper relations of literature to history. For instance, the sketch of the course of English poetry that precedes the review of Ford's *Dramatic Works* is an interesting sketch of the elementary external facts of English literary history for two centuries; but it is almost entirely without those illuminating glimpses that prove keen critical insight, and it gives you no clear notion of the ways in which the changing national life embodies itself in literature. In the instance mentioned, as in some others, the first part of the essay seems to have little connection with the rest — the introduction does not introduce. Similar comment might be made on the opening sections of the reviews of Campbell's *English Poets* and of Goethe's *Wilhelm Meister*. Such passages are of interest as showing that Jeffrey had some dawning conception of an historical method in criticism; but he hardly had more. And he seemed quite unable to apply any such method to the literature of his own day. One would have thought, for example, that in the poetry of Byron and its wonderful vogue all over Europe, Jeffrey might have seen and pointed out some significant expression of the spirit of the age; but it cannot be said that he ever did.

The other kind of introduction, that is taken up with general critical principles, is often still more disappointing. For this formidable array of truths, which would seem to make the conclusion drawn from them quite irresistible, turns out on examination to be only the generalized expression of Francis Jeffrey's personal likes and dislikes, a set of high *priori* statements all out of his own head. He always assumes himself to be the representative of those instructed few who have authority on matters of taste, and he mistakes the limitations of his own appreciation for general laws. A good many critics, I am afraid, do that; but Jeffrey shakes still more our confidence in the stability of his judgment, not merely by the jaunty facility with which he lays down general principles, but by his unlucky denial, now and

then, of some statement assumed as an eternal truth ·
only a little while before. Thus, writing in April,
1810, an elaborate review on the poetry of Crabbe,
he declares that we are all "touched more deeply
as well as more frequently in real life with the suffer-
ings of peasants than of princes . . . and an effort
to interest in the feelings of the humble and obscure
will call forth more deep, more numerous, and more
permanent emotions than can be excited by the for-
tunes of princesses and heroes"; but four months
later, having to explain the wonderful popularity of
Scott, he decides that it is mostly due to his subject,
and that "kings, warriors, knights, outlaws, min-
strels, secluded damsels and true lovers" are the sort
of persons to appeal to the general poetic sense. And
his whole *a priori* explanation of the conditions of
poetic popularity was, two years later, overset by the
meteoric fame of Byron on quite different grounds.
In the essay on Goethe's *Wilhelm Meister*, Jeffrey
declares that "human nature is everywhere funda-
mentally the same"; in the review of Baber's *Memoirs*, two years later, he decides that there is "a
natural and inherent difference in the character and
temperament of the European and Asiatic races."
One who goes straight through his essays will come
upon a considerable number of such contradictions.
Jeffrey's general principles we suspect are mostly
made to order. He first makes up his decision upon

the work under review, quite empirically, and then frames a set of universal truths to justify his decision. Mr. Leslie Stephen, indeed, goes so far as to say that Jeffrey had no real taste of his own at all, and is always asking himself, not "What do I feel?" but "What is the correct remark to make?" But this seems to me unfair. Jeffrey, I should rather say, is always asking himself "Why ought I to feel as I do?" He has a very genuine, though limited, appreciation, and is bent on justifying it.

His various likes and dislikes are curious, and often apparently irreconcilable. Yet a little reflection will show how they all spring from a common ground of temperament. Jeffrey, if I understand him, was a singular combination — I can hardly say compound — of sense and sensibility. His emotions were easy to get at; but they were checked by anything improbable, by any shock to his prosaic sense of fact. He sincerely professed enthusiastic admiration for the romantic literature of the sixteenth century, especially the Elizabethan drama, which, he says, "I have long worshipped with a kind of idolatrous veneration"; but for the romantic literature of his own day, he had a very qualified liking. Coleridge's *Ancient Mariner* seems always to have been to him nothing better than an old sailor's foolish yarn; of *Christabel* he says — or, at all events, allowed the *Edinburgh* to say, in a review always attributed to him — that "the thing is utterly destitute of value, a mixture of raving and drivelling . . . beneath criticism." His estimate of Scott was forced up by the pressure of public opinion; but of *Marmion* he could say, in 1808: "We must remind our readers that we never entertained much partiality for this sort of composition, and ventured on a former occasion to regret that an author endowed with such talents should consume them in imitation of obsolete extravagances. . . . To write a modern romance of chivalry seems to be much such a phantasy as to build a modern abbey or an English pagoda." On the other hand, for the work of Crabbe, the most merciless of realists, he always had a great admiration. Here, he said, are the facts of life. These farmers and shopkeepers and workhouse folk are the real thing; they "represent the common people of England pretty much as they are" — not as Mr. Wordsworth's philosophical peddlers, and sententious leech-gatherers, and hysterical school masters. In a word, Jeffrey liked romanticism, — as he understood it, — and he liked realism; but he did not like them mixed. The romantic writers, he would say, may fairly abandon the present and the actual; but to throw the hues of imagination on the facts of common life, as Wordsworth attempted to do, this was merely to falsify the facts without illuminating them.

So, too, he objects to the conventional poetic diction of the eighteenth century on precisely the same grounds as Wordsworth in his famous preface, and sometimes in almost the same words. He praises Cowper without stint as the first to abandon that diction and to break away from all rigid poetic convention. Yet not the most finical classicist of the eighteenth century could have had greater dread of anything rude or undignified. Wordsworth's simplicity he accounts vulgar and puling; and he shudders politely over such very mild improprieties as the guard-room talk of the soldiers in the *Lady of the Lake*. One wonders how he would have survived a reading of — let us say — some of Rudyard Kipling's ballads. The one poet most entirely to his liking was Campbell, always proper and always sentimental. "We rejoice," he says, in opening his review of the *Gertrude of Wyoming*, "to see once more a polished and pathetic poem;" though he fears it may not appeal to the taste of an age "vitiated by babyishness" (*i.e.* of Wordsworth) "or antiquarism" (*i.e.* of Scott). In a famous passage in one of the very latest of his papers — quoted by everybody who has written anything on Jeffrey since Christopher North quoted it first in *Blackwood* — looking backward over a generation, he concludes that Keats, Shelley, Wordsworth, Crabbe, are already passing into oblivion; Scott's novels have put out his poetry; even the splendid strains of Moore are fading into distance and dimness, and the blazing star of Byron receding from its place of pride; while the two poets who still keep the laurels fresh with no signs of fading are — Rogers and Campbell!

All of which proves, not that Jeffrey had no taste of his own, but that it was narrowed in its range, on the one hand by a hard common sense, and on the other by a rather prim sentimentality. It was his misfortune that, with his limited critical equipment, he had to deal with two or three very original poets, innovators who broke new paths for themselves. Of Shelley he never ventured any estimate at all. The great *Edinburgh* criticism of Shelley was written by Hazlitt. Byron for a time quite dazed him, as he dazed everybody. Before that overmastering genius, even Jeffrey's insistent common sense was blinded. He holds his breath over the magniloquence of Manfred, and avers that the dialogue which to so many of us now seems the veriest bathos is "so exquisitely managed that all sense of its impossibility is swallowed up in beauty." The worst fault of Manfred he declares to be, not that it is hollow and theatric, but that it "fatigues and overawes us with terror and sublimity." He has doubtless suffered most from his judgment of Wordsworth. Yet to-day the most enthusiastic Wordsworthian must admit that there is a good deal of solemn rubbish in Wordsworth, and not a little puerility. Nobody is obliged to read the whole of the *Excursion;* while as for *Goody Blake* and *Harry Gill, Alice Fell, Peter Bell,* and some dozen or more of that family, no one need much care to save them from the jaws of devouring Time. Our quarrel with Jeffrey is that he is not content to say of the *Excursion,* as Bottom says of the play, "There are things in this that will never please," but he must go on to pick out for special reprobation some of the very best passages in the poem. So in his flings at Wordsworth's simplicity, scattered through various essays, — as those on Crabbe and on Burns, — he points his ridicule by mentioning just the verses dearest to the lovers of Wordsworth, as the *Leech-Gatherer,* the *Matthew* poems, *Michael,* and what he calls "the stuff about dancing daffodils." The truth is that to the practical, mundane intelligence of Jeffrey all the most characteristic excellences of Wordsworth's poetry were quite invisible. Wordsworth's feeling of an all-pervading spiritual power in nature, his resulting conviction of the direct influence of nature upon character, his notion of the effect of the imagination on moral culture, — all this to Jeffrey was mere mystical nonsense. Wordsworth's subjective treatment of humble life, that, he thought, was a whimsical falsification of fact. There were no such plain people. He could not see it was not the peasant that made the poem, but Wordsworth's thought about the peasant. Wordsworth's poetical theories may have been right or may have been wrong; but before he condemned them Jeffrey should have understood them.

In briefest summary, then, we may admit that to Jeffrey, rather than to any other man, may be given the credit of raising the critical essay to the rank of a recognized literary form; that his writing is always brilliant and plausible; that his critical verdicts are always clear, and if upon matters within the range of his appreciation, sensible and just. On the other hand, it must also be admitted that his range of appreciation is limited; that his impressions are often worth more than the dogmas he invents to justify them; and that a considerable part of his fame was due to the immense and novel popularity of the Review which raised him for a time to literary dictatorship almost like that of Dryden or Johnson.

III

But important as was the service of the two great Reviews in calling out a new variety of literature, the most entertaining prose written in England between 1800 and 1825 is not to be found in their pages. The men whose work we have to consider in this volume contributed but little to the Reviews, and none of

their best. The reason is obvious. The Review
did not invite that kind of writing out of which
the best literature is made. It was not essays
they wanted, but extended reviews of contemporary
questions, suggested by some current book or books.
Within such limitations there was little opportunity
for original and creative work, or even for that play
of personal feeling, that intimate and subjective
note, which so often gives to writing permanent literary charm. The whimsical humors of Lamb, the
causeries of Hazlitt, the rambling reminiscences of
De Quincey, the jovial " Noctes" of Wilson, — they
would each and all have been out of place in the dignified pages of the *Edinburgh* or *Quarterly*. Moreover, both Reviews had provoked the most violent
antagonism of some of the best contemporary writers. Neither De Quincey nor Lamb could ever
forgive the *Edinburgh* its vituperation of Wordsworth and Coleridge, the gods of their early idolatry;
while to Hazlitt, the mere mention of Gifford and the
Tory *Quarterly* was a red rag to set him roaring,
and the *Edinburgh*, with its timid Whiggism and
dread of all radicalism, seemed to him but little better.
Much of the work of these men, therefore, found
publication, not in the Reviews but in the new Magazines. The father of all English Magazines was the
Gentleman's Magazine, founded by Edward Cave
in 1731, and followed before 1800 by several other

23

periodicals of similar character. All these Magazines, however, as their name implied, were repositories for miscellaneous matter — summaries of recent news with brief comment, excerpts from current literature or from rare or curious books, expositions of difficult or obscure passages in the classics or in Scripture, bits of odd and striking fact and incident. They afforded scanty room for original writing of any sort. Perhaps the most noteworthy contribution to them before 1800 was those famous reports of parliamentary debates written by Sam Johnson, mostly out of his own head. But in 1814 the *New Monthly Magazine* was established under the editorship of the poet Campbell; three years later appeared that more famous periodical, *Blackwood's Magazine*, which at once rivalled the Reviews in popularity and influence. In 1821 the *London Magazine* was started by John Scott, — the brilliant young critic who fell in a duel next year, — with Charles Lamb announced as one of its principal contributors. These new Magazines were entirely unlike the dreary publications of that name in the preceding century. The new Reviews had vastly raised the character and repute of periodical writing; to write for them now brought fame with the public and hard cash from the publisher. This high standard the new Magazines maintained. They commanded the pens of the most brilliant and am-

bitious young men. Published not quarterly but
monthly, they were fresher and more vigorous than
the Reviews; open to good writing on all subjects,
they invited papers more varied, original, imaginative, than could find admission to the Reviews. Under such encouragement we get a new type of essay.
The essays of Hazlitt, De Quincey, and Lamb combine the personal, intimate charm of Addison's best
work with a more highly elaborated form and a
much wider range of interest. There is no type of
literature more altogether delightful; and there are
no better specimens of the type than in the work of
the writers we have to consider in the following pages.

WILLIAM HAZLITT

I

ANY sketch of William Hazlitt may fitly begin with an extract from his most familiar essay — the most delightful essay of personal reminiscence in the English language. It is the story of his spiritual birth.

"My father was a dissenting minister, at Wem, in Shropshire; and in the year 1798 (the figures that compose the date are to me like the 'dreaded name of Demogorgon') Mr. Coleridge came to Shrewsbury to succeed Mr. Rowe in the spiritual charge of a Unitarian congregation there. He did not come till late on the Saturday afternoon before he was to preach; and Mr. Rowe, who himself went down to the coach in a state of anxiety and expectation, to look for the arrival of his successor, could find no one at all answering the description but a round-faced man, in a short black coat (like a shooting jacket) which hardly seemed to have been made for him, but who seemed to be talking at a great rate to his fellow-passengers. Mr. Rowe had scarce returned to give an account of his disappointment, when the round-faced man in black entered, and dissipated all doubts on the subject by beginning to talk. He did not cease while he stayed; nor has he since, that I know of. He held the good town of Shrewsbury in delightful suspense for three weeks that he remained there, 'fluttering the proud Salopians like an eagle in a dove-cote,' and the Welsh mountains that skirt the horizon with their tempestuous confusion, agree to have heard no such mystic sounds since the days of

" 'High-born Hoel's harp or soft Llewellyn's lay.'

As we passed along between Wem and Shrewsbury, and I eyed their blue tops seen through the wintry branches, or the red rustling leaves of the sturdy oak trees by the roadside, a sound was in my ears as of a Syren's song; I was stunned, startled with it, as from deep sleep; but I had no notion then that I should ever be able to express my admiration to others in motley imagery or quaint allusion, till the light of his genius shone into my soul, like the sun's rays glittering in the puddles of the road."

And then follows the account of Coleridge's sermon, next day: —

"For myself, I could not have been more delighted if I had heard the music of the spheres. Poetry and Philosophy had met together. Truth and Genius had embraced, under the eye and with the sanction of religion. This was even beyond my hopes. I returned home well satisfied. The sun that was still laboring, pale and wan, through the sky, obscured by thick mists, seemed an emblem of the *good cause;* and the cold dank drops of dew, that hung half melted on the beard of the thistle, had something genial and refreshing in them; for there was a spirit of hope and youth in all nature, that turned everything into good."

It is dangerous to begin quoting Hazlitt; one never knows when to stop. Better even than these first paragraphs are the later portions of this charming essay, describing that visit of the following spring when the young Hazlitt tramped three days through mud and mire to see the god of his idolatry at home in the Nether-Stowey cottage; was taken by Coleridge to see Wordsworth at the Alfoxden House hard by; discussed with Coleridge everything in heaven and earth, and heard Wordsworth read in solemn chant his yet unpublished *Lyrical Ballads;* lived for three exalted weeks in such companionship, returning often on evenings from Alfoxden to Stowey by the lovely wooded walk, when the nightingale sang in the leafage, the stream that slipped through the green glimmered in the moonlight, and Coleridge's voice sounded on

"Of Providence, foreknowledge, will and fate,
Fix'd fate, free will, foreknowledge absolute."

28

The whole picture still glows in Hazlitt's pages with the color of his early hope and dream. Nothing that the poets themselves wrote in that *annus mirabilis*, 1798–1799, not even the diary of Dorothy Wordsworth for those months, can bring the local habitation, the homely life and high thinking of Coleridge and Wordsworth, so vividly to the imagination as this paper of Hazlitt's.

At the time of this memorable visit Hazlitt was just completing his twentieth year. At first thought it may not be quite clear why he always acknowledged such great obligation to Coleridge; for his own mind had by this time already taken its bent, and he had a full set of radical opinions, if not yet quite made, at least in the making.

His radicalism he came honestly by. Dissent and revolt, both political and religious, ran in the blood of his family. An elder brother of his father had early migrated to America, heartily espoused the cause of the American rebels, and served with distinction through the Revolutionary War. Hazlitt's father had been educated in Glasgow University for a Presbyterian minister; but he soon developed a more pronounced liberalism, and before he began preaching he had become a Unitarian. A radical in politics also, he formed the acquaintance of Benjamin Franklin, and during all the period of the American difficulties found himself in hearty sympathy with the cause his brother had espoused. After the conclusion of peace he came over to America himself with his family, minded to pass his life in the new republic where liberty had taken up her seat. He did reside for more than a year in Philadelphia, and gave a course of lectures in the University of Pennsylvania; thence he removed to the vicinity of Boston, in which city he is said to have organized the first Unitarian society in America. But Unitarianism could not yet make much headway against Puritan orthodoxy; and no congregation would quite venture to give the young English preacher a settlement. We may surmise, too, that his studious and retiring temper found the atmosphere of our New England society rather raw. At all events he returned to England in the summer of 1787, and shortly after settled in the little parish of Wem, in Shropshire. Here he lived all the rest of his days, "repining but resigned," says his son, "far from the only two things he loved — talk about disputed texts of Scripture, and the cause of civil and religious liberty." A fine type of the learned, rational dissenter, this elder Hazlitt, in the tiny study at Wem, surrounded by his tall folios, or in the garden gathering "broccoli plants and kidney beans of his own rearing," his imagination far away in dreams of patriarchal eld, yet now and then waking to some stout utterance in behalf of tolerance and liberty to-day. He survived to the venerable age of eighty-four; and when the end came, says his daughter, "he made no complaint, nor did he give one groan, but went on talking of glory, honor, and immortality to the end." From him his son inherited, along with his speculative, introspective habit, a certain largeness of imagination and a sense of the high solemnities of life. When Hazlitt's writing is at its very best, we may feel in its stately rhythm and its sublime imagery the moving of his father's spirit.

It was, however, the father's love of civil and religious liberty that showed earliest in the young Hazlitt. His first printed article, a letter to a Shrewsbury newspaper in 1791, was an indignant rebuke of the intolerant churchmen who sympathized with the Birmingham mob that had just burned down the house of Dr. Priestley. The breadth of view and force of statement in this paper, by a boy of thirteen, was very remarkable. The years from fourteen to twenty-one are probably the determining period of every man's life. For Hazlitt they certainly were. Like so many men of generous temper, he had fallen under the spell of the French Revolution, which was unrolling its stupendous drama during just those years from 1792 to 1799, when his opinions were a-forming. Before he was seventeen he had drawn out a scheme of civil and criminal legislation based on the most doctrinaire notions of individual rights.

For three or four years, thereafter, he was striving in vain to put into satisfactory literary shape a treatise on the *Principles of Human Action* which should prove "the natural disinterestedness of human nature." The central thesis of this speculation he conceived to be an important discovery of his own — certainly it would be important, if true. But the course of history in those years, one thinks, must have strained his theory rather severely sometimes. The early excesses and atrocities of the Revolution, the worst of which occurred while he was in his early teens, could not change his convictions, but (though there is no record of his experience in those years) I suspect they did sometimes becloud his enthusiasm. Indeed, Hazlitt was always distrustful of enthusiasm. He had no liking for the raw multitude, and all his days had some trouble to keep his sympathies on good terms with his principles. He confessed, later in life, that he had been staggered in his devotion to republicanism and puritanism, when he reflected that, though there was plenty of both in America, it was yet doubtful whether in all the United States, from Boston to Baltimore, — his geography wouldn't let him go farther south, — we could produce a single head like one of Titian's noblemen, nurtured in all the pride of aristocracy and all the blindness of popery. He never shared Wordsworth's interest in humble folk, and declared that those Cumberland

32

ploughmen and peddlers were low company that, for himself, he did not care to meet. Ignorance is always bad enough, he said, but rustic ignorance is intolerable. Nor did the fact that common folk were hardly treated suffice to make them interesting. "Never pity people," he says, "because they are ill-used; they only wait the opportunity to use others just as ill." Hate the oppressor and prevent the evil if you can, but do not fancy there is any virtue in being oppressed. The unfortunate are not a jot more amiable than their neighbors. Such cynical sentiments, to be sure, come from the later years of disillusion; but Hazlitt was never really a democrat. He always hated the kings more than he loved the peoples.

With this temper it is not difficult to understand how, by 1798, his political devotion had already begun to fix itself upon Napoleon Bonaparte. By the beginning of the nineteenth century Napoleon had crushed the sanguinary factions of the Revolution into order; he had raised the young French republic out of chaos to a pitch of eminence above the highest dream of Richelieu; he had liberated Italy — or said he had; he had shaken every throne on the continent, and stood for the moment before all the world, the foe of all the elder tyranny, the champion of an ordered, victorious liberty. Here was a noble figure, "who nothing common did nor mean"; worthy to march at the front of the new age. For William Hazlitt, he was ever thereafter the hero who had broken up the old order, the protagonist in the cause of the Peoples against the Divine Right of Kings.

And it was for somewhat analogous reasons that the young Hazlitt welcomed Coleridge so gladly. In those years he was an eager student of the best things in letters; but here again he found a clash between his tastes and his principles. The ablest contemporary literature, the eloquence, the imagination, he had to own, were on the wrong side. He was quick enough to see that incomparably the best prose written in his time was in Burke's great pamphlet against the French Revolution. "From the first time I ever cast my eye on anything of Burke's," he writes, "I said to myself, this is true eloquence. All other styles seemed to me pedantic or infinitesimal; Burke's was forked and playful as the lightning." The doctrine was all wrong, but how immensely superior as literature was this heresy to the frigid sermons, the meagre and acrid pamphlets of the other party. It was then that he met Coleridge. Here, at last, was the orator, the philosopher, the poet — and on the side of the angels! For those were the days of Coleridge young, full of all glad enthusiasm, and with a gift of speech to make the most abstruse philosophy sound musical as Apollo's lute. It is easy to understand what strengthening of resolve, what stimulus to independent thinking, what large though vague ideals, this man Coleridge would give to the lonely and isolated young thinker.

Not, however, that there were any immediate results to show for it. The results were to come some twenty years later. Throughout the period of his early manhood Hazlitt was, indeed, trying hard to put his notions on paper; but without success. He averred that he had thought for eight years without being able to write a single page. This sterility was due, in part, doubtless, to his own exacting literary judgment, in part to his inexperience and the immaturity of the conceptions he was trying to express; but it was due, most of all, to the fact that he was wrestling with subjects that, nowever interesting to him at the time, were not really congenial. Hazlitt was an acute and subtle thinker, but he was never a systematic thinker. I should say that with all his fondness for speculation he never had the gift of philosophic exposition. He is delightful whenever, as in his later essays, he lets himself go; and many really profound truths of human nature slip into the stream of fancy, and sentiment, and half-cynical observation that he pours out with no care for method. In fact, he never writes well save when he is writing of himself. But in those early efforts he was trying to be impersonal and philosophic. The *Argument in Favor of the Natural Disinterestedness of the*

Human Mind, — which did not get published until 1805, — unlike his later work, is dry as a remainder biscuit. If Hazlitt found it difficult to write, we find it quite as difficult to read. Nor do the philosophers have much to say for it. The central theme of the treatise Hazlitt thought to be an important discovery of his own; namely, that there is no such thing "as an innate and necessary selfishness." Which may or may not be true, Hazlitt's argument thereupon not being lucid to the non-metaphysical mind; but as he admits "a practical self-interest arising out of habit and circumstances" which may serve as well as the innate article, the "discovery" would not seem very startling. Hazlitt himself always had a fondness for the book, — I suppose because it had cost him so much labor, — and he reworked the substance of it in two of his later essays.

Hopeless of success in literature, Hazlitt tried art. His elder brother was a portrait painter of some promise, and he resolved to adopt the same profession. In 1802, after the peace of Amiens, he went over to Paris to study in the Louvre, just then enriched by Napoleon's plunder from all the galleries of Europe. But in this art, too, he felt his powers fell far short of his ideals, and about 1806, after years of patient effort, he laid down his brush. Yet those years were, perhaps, among the most profitable of his life. He was not only preparing himself to be as good a critic of art as of literature, but he was gaining a delicacy of perception and a keenness of appreciation for all the outward charm of the world that was to make him one of the most picturesque of writers. And it is perhaps not fanciful to say that his constant endeavor as a portrait painter to read the *meaning* of faces had something to do with his remarkable power in the analysis and interpretation of character, shown in his later writings.

But whatever the profit of those years of apprenticeship to art, they certainly were the happiest years of Hazlitt's life. No one can read his delightful essay *On the Pleasures of Painting* without feeling that he was doing what he loved to do. For he loved to live by himself, with the companionship of those forms of nature and those works of art that will not quarrel nor betray. His work as a painter called him out of the temper of irritation to which he was naturally inclined, out of the meaner accompaniments of controversy, and gave him for a time a certain poise and quiet. For beauty always has one advantage over truth as an object of contemplation — you know it when you see it; you cannot doubt or dispute over it.

Hazlitt's mind was ripening in all ways during the years from 1798 to 1808; by the end of that decade it had got its growth. The thirty or forty books

that were to be his life-long companions — Shakespeare, Milton, Rousseau, the eighteenth-century
English essayists and writers, to name only those
he liked most — he had got by heart; for the rest
of his life he kept on reading them over and over.
He used to say in later life that he had not read a
new book since he was thirty. His political notions,
too, had taken their final shape, and had subtly
linked themselves with the brightest memories of
that golden time. In the essay *On the Pleasures
of Painting* he tells us with a thrill of longing and
recollection how he finished one of his first portraits
on the day which brought news of the battle of
Austerlitz.

"I walked out in the afternoon, and as I returned,
saw the evening star set over a poor man's cottage,
with other thoughts and feelings than I shall ever
have again. Oh, for the revolution of the great
Platonic year, that those days might come over again!
I could gladly sleep out the intervening 365,000
years!"

One thinks, by contrast, of the great Pitt, on hearing the same news, saying in despair, "Fold up the
map of Europe," and sinking back to die. To the
statesman it was the dark close of a great chapter
of history; to the young painter the triumphal
opening of a new one. In fact, I think one reason
why Hazlitt held so obstinately to his opinions was

that they had been identified with his purest sentiments, hallowed by a thousand of the dearest associations of his youth. To deny or change them
seemed treachery to the best impulses of his best
years.

Just what Hazlitt was doing for several years after
he gave up painting, is not very clear. His home,
up to about 1808, seems to have been with his
father at Wem; but he was much in London, and in
1805 he had formed the acquaintance of his best
friend, Charles Lamb. For the next twenty years
it was at this quiet bachelor fireside of Charles and
Mary Lamb that he found his tongue loosened to
say his best and brightest things. He soon met all
of Lamb's set, — Godwin, Burney, Manning, Rickman, Dyer, and the rest, — and though he was too
shy and moody to be a "clubable man," his face
came to be familiar at Lamb's Wednesday nights,
and in some fortunate hours he could be the most
brilliant of the company. Mary said he was orna-
mental as a Wednesday man, but he was more useful
on common days, when he dropped in after a quarrel
or a fit of the glooms. He had no desire to extend
the circle of his acquaintance, especially in that half
of society a young man of twenty-seven might have
been thought most willing to know. Lamb writes
to Wordsworth in 1806: "W. Hazlitt is in town.
I took him to see a very pretty girl professedly,

where there were two young girls — the very head and sum of the Girlery was two young girls — they neither laughed, nor sneered, nor giggled, nor whispered—but they were young girls — and he sat and frowned blacker and blacker, indignant that there should be such a thing as Youth and Beauty, till he tore me away before supper in perfect misery, and owned that he could not bear young girls. They drove him mad. So I took him home to my old nurse, where he recovered perfect tranquillity. Independent of this, and as I am not a young girl myself, he is a great acquisition to us." [1]

In 1808, however, the misogynist, having no visible means of support, married — having first written a refutation of the doctrines of Malthus. The lady was Miss Sarah Stoddard, a friend of the Lambs, who apparently had not enough of either youth or beauty to frighten Hazlitt's shyness. Miss Stoddard was the kind of a woman spoken of with awe as "of superior ability"; well emancipated, strong of mind and body. She had, moreover, some eighty pounds a year, while Hazlitt, as Lamb said, had only what he could claim from the parish. In addition to her income she had a Lilliputian estate at Winterslow, near Salisbury, and there the newly married couple took up their residence. Four years later, however, in 1812, finding it necessary to

[1] June 26, 1806.

do something for the support of his family, Hazlitt came up to London, and spent most of his after life there. Yet he always had a fondness for Winterslow. A lonely wayside inn on the edge of the heath, a mile from the village, was the refuge to which, in all his later years, he would flee when vexed by society or craving solitude for work. His very best writing was done there.

On coming up to London, Hazlitt obtained a position on the *Chronicle* newspaper, first as reporter and then as theatrical critic. But it was Leigh Hunt's *Examiner* that enabled him to find his genius. In 1814 Hunt projected a series of essays in the easy manner of Addison which should deal with the humors, the foibles, the philosophy of daily life. In these papers, afterward collected under the title *The Round Table*, Hazlitt first opened that delightful personal vein in which all his best work is done. His drudgery on the *Chronicle* had shown him that he could write when he must; now for the first time he found it easy to write. He was morbidly shy and reserved in company, but for that very reason the most unreserved of authors with the pen. The man who doesn't dare to take himself for granted in society is just the most communicative in his study. He isn't talking to you, he is talking to himself — and talking about himself. There is criticism, and satire, and fancy, and philosophy in what Hazlitt

41

writes; but it is all in the first person, all passed through the medium of his own feeling. It is William Hazlitt pouring himself out on paper.

After the appearance of the *Table Talk* Hazlitt was sure of an audience and a publisher, and might have been secure from pecuniary embarrassment, had he not always obeyed somewhat too literally the Scripture injunction to take no thought for the morrow. In the fifteen years that remained to him he produced a very considerable body of literature. The best of it is in the volumes entitled *Table Talk* and *The Plain Speaker*, and in similar papers contributed to various periodicals, and collected by his son under the title *Sketches and Essays*. In 1818 he gave two courses of literary lectures on the English Comic Writers and on the English Poets; and in the following year a third course on the Dramatic Literature of the Age of Elizabeth. These essays and lectures, with some other critical and miscellaneous writing, fill twelve rather stodgy volumes in the latest edition of his works. To these we must add what he himself deemed his *magnum opus*, the *Life of Napoleon*, upon which he lavished the toil of his last years.

The life of Hazlitt, after he had once found his pen and his place, is without noteworthy external incident, if we except those growing out of his domestic infelicity. That is not a pretty, nor — for us — a very important story. What perverse fate induced William Hazlitt and Sarah Stoddard to marry, no man can tell; though doubtless Miss Stoddard could have given a syllogism for it — she was of that sort. But Hazlitt said in a charming essay, "I love myself without a reason; I would have my wife do so, too." Lamb thought there was some love on both sides at first, but apparently not enough to last long. There was never any violent rupture, still less any jealousy on either side or any cause for it; but the very unconventional ways of Mrs. Hazlitt evidently got on her husband's nerves a good deal, while to a woman of her large, red health such a man as Hazlitt doubtless seemed a poor creature. After 1819 they lived mostly apart, and in 1822, by mutual consent, went up to Edinburgh to make the forty days' residence there necessary for a divorce under the Scottish law. Mrs. Hazlitt's journal during this time shows a remarkable superiority to considerations of sentiment. Hazlitt himself, meantime, during one of his periods of bachelor residence in London, had fallen very precipitously in love with a certain Sarah Walker, the daughter of a tailor in whose house he was lodging. Probably a little flattered and a little bewildered by the attentions of so singular a character, the girl did not at once refuse them, and Hazlitt's regard passed at once into something like insanity. Miss Walker,

43

however, had sense enough to see that marriage with him would be folly; while he was in Edinburgh she refused to correspond with him, and when he returned to London, a separated man, he found that she had wisely transferred her regard to an earlier and younger suitor. Hazlitt thereupon sat down and put the whole story of his passion into a book, which in its astonishing frankness quite out-Rousseaus Rousseau. The *Liber Amoris* (which Mr. Le Gallienne took needless trouble to rescue from oblivion in a reprint some years ago) is not exactly a bad book — there was nothing base in Hazlitt's infatuation; but in its vulgar lack of all reserve it is nearly as unpleasant reading as some of our modern decadent novels. To say the truth, there is, not only here but occasionally elsewhere in Hazlitt's explosions of petulance or of sentiment, something a little under-bred. He hadn't quite the dignified reticence of a gentleman. Sarah Walker — having once "cleansed his stuffed bosom of that perilous stuff" by publishing the *Liber Amoris* — he speedily forgot. Next year, 1824, he married a certain Mrs. Bridgewater, of whom nothing particular is known save she had three hundred pounds a year. On this Hazlitt took the continental journey he had long coveted, to Paris (where he met the first Mrs. Hazlitt and gave her some of the second Mrs. Hazlitt's money), to Genoa, Florence, and Rome. The last part of his wedding journey, however, he seems to have taken alone; and when, on his return to England next year, he wrote to his wife asking her to join him, she replied that they were now separated forever. From that time Hazlitt led a rather hermit-like life in London and in the Hut at Winterslow, writing occasionally for the magazines and for the *Edinburgh*, and toiling hard at his *Life of Napoleon*. His health, injured perhaps by his habit of drinking enormous quantities of strong tea, began to break, and he died in 1830, at the age of fifty-two.

II

Hazlitt's last words were, "Well, I have had a happy life." This certainly seems at first blush a strange verdict upon a life full of disappointment and complaint. For Hazlitt had never mastered the art of living with men, still less the art of living with woman. His best friends found him sometimes very difficult. He was morbidly timid and suspicious by nature. De Quincey says that if Hazlitt left some friend in a room for a few minutes, on his return he would look about him with a mixed air of suspicion and defiance as if challenging something that had been said against him in his absence. Leigh Hunt used to describe a shake of his hand as something like a fish tendering you his fin. His face wore habitually a half-sad, half-angry look, over which some high thought or noble feeling would throw a sudden flash as of a lightning gleam, then fading out again in sullen night. He knew himself the most awkward of mortals, and in one of his essays confesses that he had never been able to come through a door gracefully. In an admirable letter to his son just going away to school, he says with an evident twinge of memory: "I wish you to learn Latin, French, and dancing. I would insist upon the last more particularly, because it is of the greatest consequence to your success in life."

And this moody sensitiveness was, of course, increased by the publicity that his writings brought him. His political opinions drew down upon his head the most virulent criticism from the Tory *Quarterly* and the *Blackwood*. The whiskey-drinking, swash-buckler reviewers of the *Blackwood*, especially, assailed him, after their wont, with such personal abuse that Mr. Blackwood was forced to some sort of apology, under threat of a suit for libel. Such attacks put Hazlitt into a kind of trembling, angry terror, and actually drove him for days into seclusion. Nor could he expect active sympathy from any quarter. His old friends, he felt, had been alienated by his own political consistency. The cause to which Coleridge and Wordsworth and

Southey, as well as himself, had given their allegiance a score of years before, they had now basely deserted. He hated Southey almost as heartily as he hated Wellington; and he is always lamenting over Coleridge, as over an archangel fallen. On the other hand, he distrusted all mere doctrinaire radicals and fanatics, all loud declaimers like Byron, and for such rhapsodical enthusiasts as Shelley, he had a dislike amounting to a positive contempt. Such men, he thought, had wrecked the Revolution at its beginning. As it was, he felt himself on most matters of importance in a minority of one, an Ishmaelite with every man's hand against him. The one man whom he did admire to idolatry was the one man whom all parties united to fear and to detest — Napoleon Bonaparte. Waterloo closed the chapter of his hopes. When the Congress of Vienna set up the Bourbon monarchy in France — an abomination in a desolation — and forced upon prostrate Europe the old odious doctrine of the Divine Right of Kings, Hazlitt refused any longer to look to the future. Thereafter he solaced himself with memories and with the proud consciousness of his own loyalty to a fallen cause.

"For my part, I started in life with the French Revolution, and I have lived, alas! to see the end of it. But I did not foresee this result. My sun arose with the first dawn of liberty, and I did not

think how soon both must set. The new impulse to
ardor given to men's minds imparted a congenial
warmth and glow to mine; we were strong to run a
race together, and I little dreamed that long before
mine was set, the sun of liberty would turn to blood,
or set once more in the night of despotism. Since
then, I confess, I have no longer felt myself young,
for with that my hopes fell."

This disappointment came, we shall remember,
just as his own literary career was opening, and gave
a bitter taste to all his success. Indeed he never
cared much for merely literary success. The higher
forms of creative literature he knew himself unequal
to; the reviews and essays for the magazines he considered of little permanent value. He would have
been pleased to render some signal literary service
to a cause of which he felt himself a champion
or a martyr; but the only two of his books that he
prized few people would read then and nobody reads
now, — the essay on the *Disinterestedness of the
Human Mind* and the *Life of Napoleon*. Thus dis-
appointed and embittered, he identified his disappointments with his principles, and persuaded himself that he did well to be angry. And he could be
very angry. Burke's apostasy drove him into a kind
of a frenzy: "That man . . . who has done more
mischief than perhaps any other man in the world

. . . who would have blotted out the broad, pure light of heaven because it did not first shine in at the little Gothic windows of St. Stephen's Chapel! . . ." and he goes on until his indignation fairly chokes him. Wellington had won Waterloo because he was just stupid enough to sit still and let his army do what it chose; Walter Scott, like Bacon, was the "greatest, wisest, meanest of mankind"; Gifford was a "low-bred, self-taught, servile pedant, a doorkeeper and a lacquey to learning," admirably qualified by a combination of *defects* to be the editor of the *Quarterly Review*. In some of his angry and querulous moods he manages to score about all his contemporaries. Even Lamb fell under his displeasure for a time, and Mary wished Hazlitt would not hate mankind quite so universally.

Yet, after all, I think Hazlitt's last words were not untrue. For the final impression one gets from reading him is that his life was by no means all unhappy. For one thing he must have got a good deal of pleasure out of his antipathies. Nobody liked a fight better. " Good nature," he says somewhere, "is only another name for stupidity," in nine cases out of ten mere indolence of disposition. Your really amiable people are those the world calls disagreeable — like himself. They will not weakly consent with you. They have opinions of their own, and the spirit to defend them, and are willing to sacrifice even the failings of their friends at the shrine of truth. For himself, he took care that his best friendships should not grow stagnant by long standing. He owned that he had quarrelled with all his acquaintances at one time or another, and shouldn't have liked them much unless he had. He cared little for the people who had no faults to talk about. But he enjoyed most a settled, hearty antipathy, one that would keep for a lifetime, and enlist his principles in its behalf. One of his most characteristic essays is entitled *On the Pleasures of Hating;* and it is written with gusto. Happiness, as well as virtue, he held, consists not merely in loving the good, but in hating the evil; and he could always identify the evil he hated with some pet adversary of his own. His pleasure was all the keener that he knew himself always on the unpopular side, and could taste the sweet sense of being wronged. And as there was no one his match in venomed satire, he had the peculiarly happy fortune of vanquishing his antagonist and losing his cause; and thus enjoyed at once the pride of victory and the pride of martyrdom.

In truth, no small share of the satisfaction of Hazlitt's maturer life came from a certain high, self-approving melancholy. He felt himself one of the faithful few who championed a lost cause, who despair but never surrender. He would fain withdraw from a world that misunderstood and slandered him, and cloister himself with his books and his memories to chew the cud of bitter-sweet fancy. Il Penseroso is far from being an unhappy man; and almost all his delights were well known to William Hazlitt. Such essays as *Reading Old Books, On Living to One's Self, On the Past and Future, Why Distant Objects Please, A Farewell to Essay Writing*, are the most perfect expression in modern prose writing of Milton's ideal, worthy companions of his immortally familiar verse. The charms of art and letters and music, the graver and more pensive beauties of the world about us, softened in the mellow light of memory — one sees them all in such essays, and knows that the writer could not have been altogether unhappy.

And in such essays it is easy to discover the charm of the man's personality. For Hazlitt was not a cynic, rather a sentimentalist. His sensibilities were overstrung. His shyness and suspicion, his irritability of temper, really came of an eager, timorous craving for sympathy that he never expected to find. Underneath his moods there was a hunger for affection. The few friends who really understood him, while they enjoyed his stinging satire, his subtle paradox, knew that behind the mask of this shy and moody temper the man cherished an admiration for all noble things, a love for all beautiful things; they knew that the enmity and irritation that made him difficult were often half affected, to give pungency to his criticism, while his friendships were real and abiding. The tribute of his best and most discriminating friend, Lamb, in an oft-quoted letter to Southey, is proof enough of the essential manhood of Hazlitt: "I think W. H. to be, in his natural and healthy state, one of the wisest and finest spirits breathing; so far from being ashamed of that intimacy which was between us, it is my boast that I was able for so many years to have possessed it entire; and I think I shall go to my grave without finding or expecting to find such a companion."

III

But whatever Hazlitt was as a man, he was certainly one of the most delightful of writers. Let me first except Sir Walter's novels and everything of Lamb's, and then I insist that the very best prose written in England between 1800 and 1830 is to be found in the pages of William Hazlitt. Nobody is obliged to read anybody's Complete Works. Drop out the *Liber Amoris* and most of the attempts at formal philosophical and political discussion, and there will still remain a body of Hazlitt's writing which by comparison makes De Quincey seem tumid, Wilson turgid, and Hunt vapid. Indeed I can understand, though I cannot quite share, the preference Walter Bagehot is said to have expressed for Hazlitt over Lamb. As far as mere style goes, I should hold that Hazlitt had no equal in his day. "He says things of his own in a way of his own," declared Coleridge; which is not a very inadequate description of good prose. Perhaps he had not the constructive ability for a great work, — though the *Napoleon* is very well composed, — but we have no better master of the short familiar essay. De Quincey, always unfair to Hazlitt, complained that he was never eloquent because his thoughts were "abrupt, discontinuous, non-sequacious." Perhaps he was not eloquent; eloquence is usually out of place in such writings as his, though there are many passages in these essays that, if not eloquent, are something better. But Hazlitt's writing, whether "sequacious" or not, is never without both order and movement. De Quincey had taken as his model the long-breathed, pompous English of the early seventeenth century, and refused to admire any writing that did not echo that prolonged sonorous note. Hazlitt's models — so far as he had any — were rather the essayists of the next century, Addison, Steele, Swift; and no more serviceable, idiomatic English than theirs was ever written. He has their ease and urbanity, their love of the first person singular, their gift to put themselves *en rapport* with the reader. But he has, also, what they never had, a vivid imagination and a quick sense of the romantic. He cannot announce any proposition but instantly there comes trooping about it a throng of images and examples. His style is, therefore, of necessity profuse, but it is neither diffuse nor labored. When he gets into a glow of passion or imagination, he may go on piling clause upon clause, and sometimes makes a sentence of portentous length, but his structure is simple; he has no tricks of style, and his very mannerisms are unconscious. His language is choice, but it is the speech of daily life, without a trace of preciosity. He is always spontaneous and sincere. He is certainly very extravagant now and then, especially in his abuse, and pours upon his enemy "a nice derangement of epitaphs"; but he *is* genuinely angry. For the moment he means all he says; though very likely on the next page he may relent and salve the wound he has made by some regretful memory or confession. No writing was ever less bookish; it is the voice of William Hazlitt speaking right on. Mr. Henley is so impressed with this colloquial charm as to believe that, excellent as is Hazlitt's writing, he must have talked even better than he wrote. But I doubt that. It is not of record that he talked brilliantly, save now and then when alone with Lamb or one or two other intimates. Listen-

ers put him out. I suspect he always talked best
with himself, alone with his books and his memories,
in the Hut at Winterslow.

He has been criticised for his habit of profuse
quotation. It would be a juster criticism that he
quotes very carelessly. In a lecture on Shakespeare
he remarks that "in trying to recollect any other
author we sometimes stumble, in case of failure, on a
word as good; in Shakespeare any other word but
the true one is sure to be wrong." And then, within
three pages, he quotes from Hamlet after this fashion:

> "There is a willow hanging o'er a brook
> That shows its hoary leaves in the glassy stream,"

which is what Falstaff might term "damnable
iteration." But the very freedom of his quotations,
at all events, proves them unstudied. They slip
unconsciously into his lines from the stores of his
memory; and the stuff of his own writing is so good
as not to suffer by contrast with his frequent borrow-
ings.

But though Hazlitt's style is so spontaneous, it
is never really careless or slovenly. His best work
was done rapidly, illumined by the momentary
play of allusion and the gleam of fancy best struck
out when the mind is heated and eager. Yet it
always shows that instinctive sense of phrase which
is the hall-mark of good style; and it always has

that crowning grace of prose, a good rhythm. All good writing, he says somewhere, *sounds* well when read aloud; his own bears that test. His manner, while familiar, has not only ease, but distinction. He said, with pardonable pride, in his last years, "I have written no common-place, nor a line that licks the dust." And frequently in some mood of lofty thought or mournful memory his effects of tone and rhythm are far more subtle and moving than any of De Quincey's bravura. There are such passages in the essay *On Antiquity*, — an essay that Sir Thomas Browne would have loved — in that *On the Feeling of Immortality in Youth, On Novelty and Familiarity*, and in half a score of others. Read a dozen of his essays, with their constant play of allusion, their apt — if over-abundant — quotation; their fleeting glimpses of imagination, now august, now beautiful, now pathetic, but always vivid; their brilliant, half-earnest paradox; their mild tone of melancholy reflection; their flashes of cynical satire; all flowing in a rhythm, unstudied yet varied and musical — and then you understand why many of the best masters of modern prose — Macaulay, Walter Bagehot, Robert Louis Stevenson, Augustine Birrell — have given to the style of Hazlitt their praise and the better tribute of imitation. "We are fine fellows," said Stevenson once, in despairing admiration, "but we can't write like William Hazlitt."

If we turn to the matter of his writing, it may be perhaps admitted that, outside of his literary criticism, he had not much to teach us. If a man has resolved never to change his mind, it doesn't much matter what he thinks. Hazlitt had practically left off thinking at thirty, and his opinions, therefore, had mostly stiffened into prejudices before he was fifty. His political principles had all resolved themselves into hatred of the authority of kings. On that theme he has numerous variations, and he can be infinitely entertaining in his attacks, angry or mournful, upon the enemies of the truth once delivered to William Hazlitt and Napoleon Bonaparte; but it cannot be said that he is very instructive. The final result of a quarter-century of political struggle, diplomatic scheming, and gigantic military effort, all over Europe, had been, so he thought, to send to St. Helena the one great foe of sanctified tyranny, and to force upon the world a solemn assent to that blasphemous doctrine, the Divine Right of Kings. And to this result both parties in England had contributed in about equal measure. The best statement of his attitude toward English politics after Waterloo is found in his preface to a volume of political essays collected in 1819. The Tories, of course, are the objects of his bitter hatred, the inveterate foes of popular liberty, the leaders in that opposition which had crushed the movements of revolution all over Europe, reseated a Bourbon on the throne of France, and arrayed a million of bayonets in defence of the odious doctrine of Divine Right. Yet, at all events, the Tories were to be credited with consistency. You knew what they were at. The Whigs, on the contrary, have not the courage of their convictions, or they have no convictions. To be an English Whig in the glorious days of 1688 was to be a representative of the people, that People who had deposed one King to make another, and could do it again. But now, under such sophistical teaching as that of Burke, the Whigs were substantially at one with the Tories on the only questions of importance. In the great European case of the People *vs.* the Kings, they were on the side of the Kings. "A modern Whig," says Hazlitt, bitterly, "is the fag end of a Tory . . . a Trimmer, that is, a coward to both sides of a question, who dares not be known as an honest man, but is a sort of whiffling, shuffling, cunning, silly, contemptible, unmeaning negation of the two." The two great Reviews were like opposite coaches, "that raise a great deal of dust and spatter one another with mud, but both travel on the same road and arrive at the same destination." As to the doctrinaire radicals, Godwin, Bentham, Horne Tooke, and the rest, they were little better. They really represent not the people, but each man him-

58

self and nobody else. They have each his own theory, and are bent on reforming the world by pure reason; overlooking the sentiments, affections, and prejudices of man, they cannot combine and cannot command. They furnish no principle of party cohesion, and consequently can never hope to do anything against the well-compacted forces of legitimacy and tradition. A reformer, in fact, is pretty sure to turn out a marplot. To the charge that in this condemnation he involved himself, Hazlitt would probably have assented readily enough. He knew that he had no gift for association or leadership. In the opening sentences of the preface just quoted, he says, "I am no politician, and still less can I be said to be a party man; but I have a hatred for tyranny and a contempt for its tools." His writing on political matters is, unfortunately, mostly limited to the various expressions of this hatred; and he never seemed to have any just appreciation of the great force of liberal sentiment that was gathering head in England for the twenty years after Waterloo, to culminate in the reforms of 1832.

Mr. Saintsbury, who always likes good round statement, pronounces Hazlitt the greatest critic England has yet produced. This seems to me a little extravagant; but if he will change the tense of his verb, I agree. Hazlitt was the greatest critic England had seen up to that time. The truth is, as Hazlitt himself admirably says, "Coleridge threw a great stone into the standing pool of English criticism which spattered some people with mud, but which gave a motion to the surface which has not since subsided." Coleridge's own work, of course, was mostly inchoate or fragmentary; but he certainly did give a new character and direction to criticism; and Hazlitt was first of the many critics to feel his influence. His criticism is to be found not only in his lectures on English writers, but scattered through all his miscellaneous writing, some of the best of it in passing comment or illustration. It is never formal or systematic. He repudiates over and over again the academic criticism of the eighteenth century, which judged a work of the imagination by the measuring-rod of Aristotle, often without giving us any idea of its power and charm. Montaigne — of whom he gives an admirable estimate in a single page — he avers to be the true critic, "who didn't compare books with rule and system or fall out with a book that is good for anything because all the angles on the corners are not right angles," but rather tells us what he himself likes in it. This is always Hazlitt's method. He is the first of English impressionist critics, and he is still one of the very best. Though his manner may seem sketchy or discursive, he succeeds in saying the few essential things about his author. He goes to the root of the matter. His brief comments, for example, on Addison, Steele, or Swift are better as appreciations than half an acre of academic platitude. There is a personal quality in his criticism. He writes with gusto. A book to him is not a mere academic exercise, a "piece of literature"; it is a piece of life, the voice of a man or a woman with whom it is worth while to be acquainted. Criticism thus becomes intimate, familiar. You may very often discover the essential character of a book as of a man, by some incidental question, some shrewd practical comparison of views. You want to find out, not how your book conforms to certain rules; you want to find out what it is good for. Now Hazlitt has in a remarkable degree the gift to enjoy for himself what is best in literature, and the gift to convey that enjoyment to his reader — which I take it is the chief function of criticism.

To be sure, criticism of this sort has its limitations. It is likely to be confined to the range of the critic's favorite reading. Fortunately, however, Hazlitt's taste was sound, and it was catholic. He seldom made the mistake of liking the second best better than he liked the best. I do not think his reading was exhaustive in any period of our literature. He cared little for the little men. In his lectures on

English poetry he slips hastily over the minor seven-teenth-century men, owning that with some of them — Donne, for example — he has no acquaintance. He sometimes took the dangerous risk of judging an author by a small sample. Thus all the biographies record that he once lectured on Beaumont and Fletcher and was afterwards foolish enough to let out that he had only read about a quarter of their work; but it was probably the best quarter, for the lecture is a very good one. But what I here insist on is that he had a thoroughly sympathetic appre-ciation of the best work of widely different periods. He was in hearty accord with the new romantic liking for Shakespeare and the Elizabethan drama; but at the same time he protested earnestly against the blindness of those critics who, like De Quincey, could see nothing worthy to be called poetry in Pope. In fact, the best criticism of Shakespeare, save only that of Coleridge, written in that generation, and the best estimate of Pope, so far as I know, in any genera-tion, are both to be found in the lectures of Hazlitt. It would be difficult to name any critic who has shown sufficient breadth of appreciation to estimate with equal justice such widely different poets as Shakespeare, Pope, Burns, Wordsworth, and Byron.

It is a more serious objection to the impressionist critic that he has no historical perspective. Hazlitt, it may be admitted, seldom makes any attempt to set an author in his proper surroundings or to show how the essential qualities of the literature of a period are decided, or at all events largely influenced, by political and social conditions. He was interested in the absolute value of a book, not in the forces of circumstance and environment that may have produced it. Nor could we expect him to be. The historical type of criticism is of recent growth; and its value is perhaps overestimated in these days when we tend to explain everything by the principle of evolution. For, after all, every great work of literature is differentiated from every other as the expression of a unique personality that cannot be predicted or explained.

But though Hazlitt's critical writing is made up for the most part of his personal judgments, it should not be thought that these judgments are purely empirical or unreasoned. Quite the contrary. He knew not only what he liked, but why he liked it. His mind was prone to speculation, and while he makes no parade of critical principles, there are frequent passages of reflection in all his work which unite philosophic acumen with literary sensibility. The lecture on *Descriptive Poetry*, for example, contains an acute analysis of the charm of nature, especially as used in literature. A collection of such passages and sentences, culled from his writing, would form a very considerable body of critical dicta. His one attempt at more systematic examination of an abstract literary theme, the lecture on *The Nature of Poetry*, is, in my judgment, one of the very best contributions to that world-old discussion.

Perhaps the surest proof of a critic's ability is to be found in his verdicts upon his contemporaries. So long as he attempts little more than to explain and justify the decisions of posterity, he runs little risk of serious error; but it is quite another thing to discover genius yet unheralded, to withstand obstinate prejudice, or to refuse adulation to the reigning popular idol. Hazlitt stands this test well. In only one instance is there any pronounced dissent to-day from his judgments upon his contemporaries.[1] The *Edinburgh Review* article on Shelley (July, 1824) will always be resented by Shelleyans; we may all admit that it is deficient in sympathy. Yet something may be said for Hazlitt. Shelley, the man, his opinions, his philosophy of life, he estimated very justly. No one has better expressed the visionary quality of Shelley's thought, combined with

---

[1] I assume that the review of Coleridge's *Christabel* in the *Edinburgh Review*, September, 1816, was not written by Hazlitt. I am not unaware that the authorship of the paper is still in dispute; but for myself I can find in it no trace of Hazlitt's manner. He could be caustic enough on the character and opinions of Coleridge; but such stupid comment as this on Coleridge's poetry he never wrote. The article in my opinion is *aut Jeffrey aut diabolus*.

high sincerity of purpose and a certain lonely obsti-
nacy of will. But the poetry of such a nature Hazlitt
could not highly prize. It seemed to him deficient in
genuine human interest. Hazlitt always liked to keep
his feet on the ground; and this verse was pure vision,
a beautiful mist arising from social and political doctrines essentially untrue. We shall remember that
Mr. Matthew Arnold held a not dissimilar opinion.

It is certainly to be said in praise of Hazlitt's
contemporary criticism that it was proof against
his party spleen. He kept his prejudices out of his
verdicts most remarkably. In those days, when to be
a Liberal was to be damned without mercy by the
Quarterly and by *Blackwood*, he was always ready
to own that good might come even out of a quarterly reviewer. We have seen how he united the most
inflammatory hatred of Burke with enthusiastic
admiration for Burke's writing. Sir Walter Scott,
the hide-bound Tory aristocrat, the servile wor-
shipper of kings, he abuses through a portentous
sentence two pages long into which he has gathered
pretty nearly all the vocabulary of opprobrium;
and in the same essay he fairly goes into rapture over
the Waverley Novels — the worst of them, he says, is
better than any other person's best, and all together
they are a new edition of human nature. Wordsworth, the solid, conservative stamp-distributor, who
sat in the Lake District solemnly admiring his own

moral being, was the butt of some of his keenest
satire; but the very best and most discriminating
criticism of Wordsworth's poetry between 1815 and
1825 was written by Hazlitt; indeed, I hardly know
of any better since. Even Southey, the renegade
laureate of George the Fourth, with his absurd
Kehamas and *Visions of Judgment*, Hazlitt praises
generously — though perhaps always with a tinge
of irony — as one of the best of prose-writers and
admirable of men, as virtuous as though there were
no cakes and ale. It was Lamb who said (and all
critics after him) that Hazlitt was more just in his
praise than in his blame; the truth seems to be that
he was just to literary excellence wherever he found
it. It was only the dull pretenders like Gifford,
whose politics and literature were alike intolerable,
that provoked his unmixed hatred.

But the most interesting, and I think the most
valuable, part of Hazlitt's work is to be found, not in
his criticism, but in the miscellaneous essays in
the *Table Talk*, the *Winterslow Essays*, the *Round
Table*, the *Plain Speaker*. These essays are so
varied in subject that it is not easy to describe them,
but they all have this in common: they are subjective and autobiographical. Hazlitt is drawing
directly upon his own experience. In this, by the
way, he is doing just what his contemporaries were

doing. That was the period of egotism in English literature. Not only the prose men, — Hazlitt, De Quincey, Lamb, — but even more noticeably the great poets, — Wordsworth, reverently detailing through eight thousand lines the growth of his mind; Byron, bearing over Europe the pageant of his bleeding heart; Shelley, panting with alternate aspiration and despair, — every one of them "looked in his heart and wrote." Scott alone had some dramatic gift and could find his themes outside himself. The value of such self-revelation depended, obviously, upon the self revealed. In the personality of Hazlitt there is certainly no lack of interest. We see in his essays an intellect disciplined and broadened by long thought, enriched by the best reading and by early and intimate acquaintance with two or three of the ablest men of that generation; a vivid imagination and a quick eye for beauty; a temper flashing into anger at opposition or softened to melancholy by failure, yet constant to the ideals of youth; a vein of perversity which always liked the back side of a truth and the under side of a quarrel; and a gift of phrase ranging from caustic epigram to lofty eloquence. And in his egotism there is no Byronic posing nor any braggart quality; it is frank, naïve, almost unconscious.

Some of these miscellaneous essays are on philosophic themes; as, *Why Distant Objects Please, On*

Personal Identity, On the Past and Future, On the Feeling of Immortality in Youth. Yet they are as genuinely autobiographical as the others. There is keen penetration, subtle analysis in plenty, but mixed with Hazlitt's sardonic humor, colored by his personal feelings, illustrated from his own experience. He was always fond of speculation upon the laws of conduct. He said that he had left off reading at an early age; but he had been watching the human comedy intently all his days, and his power of psychological analysis was very acute. He likes to expose the unfamiliar side of some familiar truth, to break up our self-satisfied commonplace, to explode a paradox under some smug propriety. He has in memory rich stores of example, and he constantly enlivens an abstract discussion with some shrewd bit of observation or bright gleam of fancy. In this subtle, imaginative, half-cynical philosophy of everyday life no other English essayist is so great a master. His pages sparkle with truths of character and conduct cast into striking aphorisms or epigrams, often with an edge of satire.

"We enjoy a friend's society only in proportion as he is satisfied with ours."

"To *look down* upon anything seemingly implies a greater elevation and enlargement of view than to *look up* to it."

"An excess of modesty is, in effect, an excess of pride."

"Fashion is gentility running away from vulgarity and afraid of being overtaken by it."

"A woman's attachment to her husband is not to be suspected if she will allow no one to abuse him but herself."

"There appears to be no natural necessity for evil, but that there is a perfect indifference to good without it.'

"We never do anything well until we cease to think about the manner of doing it."

"An Englishman is sure to speak his mind more plainly than others — yes, if it will give you more pain to hear it."

Such pithy statements were not carefully studied for rhetorical effect. Hazlitt was never ambitious of mere smartness. But he did like to put the extreme case, to show some fact of human nature in unfamiliar and unexpected relations. He confesses a tendency to "chase my ideas into paradox or mysticism." For a paradox is not a falsehood which seems true, but a truth that seems false; and in that guise it often gains admission where truth in homespun commonplace would be ignored or turned away.

But the most striking and characteristic passages in these philosophical essays are those in which Hazlitt — to use his phrase again — chases . his idea, not into paradox, but into mysticism. He was always haunted by some sense of the mystery that touches our practical life at every point, the unfathomable depth of meaning in our common speech. At the suggestion of a simple incident or familiar word, he may pass into a mood of solemn wonder and imagining. Thus, for example, the problem of the essential nature of Time, the little instant marked off for each of us as by the bounds of Birth and Death from the Eternities, had always a strange fascination for him. "That things should be that are now no more, creates in my mind," he says, "the most profound astonishment. I cannot solve the mystery of the past, nor exhaust my pleasure in it." In his moods of reflection upon this world-old mystery, though he never preached, his writing takes on a solemn yet impassioned dignity of movement and imagery that sets it beside our very noblest prose. Such a sentence as this, with its heaped-up statement of all the possibilities of life suddenly smitten across by the stroke of annihilation, reminds us of Jeremy Taylor.

"To see the golden sun, the azure sky, the outstretched ocean; to walk upon the green earth and be lord of a thousand creatures; to look down yawning precipices or over distant sunny vales; to see the world spread out under one's feet as a map; to bring the stars near; to view the smallest insects through a

microscope; to read history, and consider the revo-
lutions of empire and the successions of generations;
to hear of the glory of Tyre, of Sidon, of Babylon,
of Susa, and to say all these were before me, and are
now nothing; to say I exist in such a point of time,
and in such a point of space; to be a spectator and a
part of its ever moving scene; to witness the change
of season, of spring and autumn, of winter and summer; to feel hot and cold, pleasure and pain, beauty
and deformity, right and wrong; to be sensible to
the accidents of nature; to consider the mighty
world of eye and ear; to listen to the stock-dove's
notes amid the forest deep; to journey over moor and
mountain; to hear the midnight sainted choir; to
visit lighted halls, or the cathedral's gloom, or sit in
crowded theatres and see life itself mocked; to study
the works of art, and refine the sense of beauty to
agony; to worship fame, and dream of immortality;
to look upon the Vatican, and to read Shakespeare;
to gather up the wisdom of the ancients, and to pry
into the future; to listen to the trump of war, the
shout of victory; to question history as to the movements of the human heart; to seek for truth; to
plead the cause of humanity; to overlook the world
as if time and nature poured their treasures at our
feet, — to be and to do all this, and then in a moment
to be nothing — to have it all snatched from us as by
a juggler's trick or a phantasmagoria!"

The most entertaining of all the essays, however, and probably the most familiar, are in a still more intimate, personal manner. Sometimes they are made up entirely of reminiscence, like the familiar essay on *My First Acquaintance with Poets*, quoted at the beginning of this paper, or that well-known account of the evening in Lamb's chambers, *On People One would Wish to have Seen*. But more frequently Hazlitt takes a topic that starts some train of reflection or gratifies some pet animosity, and talks a half-hour, *On Reading Old Books, On the Look of a Gentleman, On Disagreeable People, On the Pleasures of Hating*, or on *Painting*. You do not go to such writing as this for instruction or for inspiration; but instruction is usually a bore, and what professes to be inspiration is often only irritation. Yet Hazlitt's papers are never made up of languid revery or idle gossip. He is always giving some sudden fillip to your thinking. This writing is a revelation of an active, nervous mind. The familiar relations of society, the old anxieties, affections, hopes, and disappointments of common life, he sets in picturesque circumstance, and invests them all with his own emotion. These essays are his criticism of life. And not by any means an altogether unwholesome criticism of life, I should say. Doubtless his predominant moods are not buoyant or optimistic. He enjoys poor health, and is a little over-severe on

the red, rotund, thick-skinned, average British man.
He was a little too much inclined to make a virtue
of his own aversions, and to mistake his own suspicion and ill-nature for stern fidelity to principle.
"No good-natured man," he says, "was ever martyr
to a cause" — like himself.   But he is always pi-
quant, original, and commands our interest for his
opinions, if not our assent.   The whims and petty
perversities that doubtless made him difficult as a
friend make him delightful as a writer.   For he was
no real cynic or misanthrope.   He kept his ideals
noble and sound.   To be sure, he had sometimes
idealized the wrong persons — Sarah Walker and
Napoleon Bonaparte, for example; and the result
was unfortunate for his temper when he discovered
his error, and unfortunate for his reputation when he
did not.   But his thoughts and memory dwelt habitually upon things honest and lovely, and of good
report.   He never jeers at virtue, and he has no cynic
scorn for his early dreams.   On the contrary, all the
best of these papers have a backward glance of fond
reminiscence.   His favorite phrase is "I remember."
He might have said with Wordsworth,

"The thought of our past years in me doth breed
  Perpetual benediction."

But with a difference.   For, out of all his memories,
Hazlitt, like Jacques (of whom I have often thought

he must have been a reincarnation), can suck melancholy as a weasel sucks eggs. It is not the mournful melancholy of a sated voluptuary, or the sour melancholy of a selfish cynic; it is the gentle regret for the early days of books and friends and hopes. He himself evidently takes a serene satisfaction in it; and it softens all his angry or querulous moods into the twilight tones of recollection. You shall not read far without coming upon some passage of genuinely poetic vision and feeling — glimpses of that kind of retreat he loved best, not rugged or remote, but in some softer solitude, as at Winterslow, hallowed by old associations, and in sound of village bells; memories of scenes he knew, or friends he loved, or books he read. He hears the sound of the curfew he heard when a boy

"Swinging slow with sullen roar,"

and the generations that are gone, the tangled forest glades and hamlets brown of his native country, the woodman's art, the Norman warrior armed for battle, the conqueror's iron rule, and the peasant's lamp extinguished, all start into memory at that clamorous peal. He recalls the time, when, in the inn at Tewksbury, he sat up the livelong night to read *Paul and Virginia;* the place where he first read Mrs. Inchbald's *Simple Story*, "while an old crazy hand-organ outside was playing *Robin Adair*, and a summer

74

shower dropped manna on my head"; or that hour
when first the great Mrs. Siddons passed before his
sight and shook his soul to tears. In such passages
his writing has all the charms of poetry save only
the accomplishment of verse.

It would be idle to claim for Hazlitt a place among
those writers who have greatly added to the knowledge, or influenced the thought, of their time. His
work is not, like that of Carlyle or Ruskin or even of
Arnold, so dominated by urgent moral purpose as to
make it an efficient spiritual force. Nor can it be
said that in the whole body of his writing there is any
one thing that for weight of thought or perfection of
structure can take highest rank as literature. But
it is safe to say that, as a master of style and as a
critic of literature, he had no superior in his own day,
and has had very few since. And his miscellaneous
writings will have a perennial charm as a storehouse
of the fancies, the humors, the poetry and wisdom,
the opinions and prejudices, the friendships and en-
mities of the man William Hazlitt. Every page is
the utterance of his unique personality. He may
have been "gey ill to live with"; but few men have
known how to write more companionable books.
Readers who ask first of all that a book shall have a
live man in it will keep his volumes always within
easy reach, on the same shelf with Elia and Boswell.

CHARLES LAMB

I

It seems idle to sit down to write an essay on Charles Lamb. As Hazlitt remarks somewhere, "There is nothing to be said respecting an author that all the world have made up their minds about." It is perhaps, also, a little dangerous, as well as idle; the average reader is likely to resent the assumption that any one is better acquainted with Elia than he is. For Charles Lamb belongs to the small group of authors for whom we cherish a kindly feeling that precludes any cool, critical estimate. They may be great writers, or they may not; they are good fellows. There are not many such. Cicero's famous praise of books that invigorate our youth and delight our age, *delectant domi, non impediunt foris, pernoctant nobiscum, peregrinantur, rusticantur*, is by no means true of all good literature. Who takes up the *Paradise Lost* to read in that half-hour before he blows out his bedside candle, or tucks the *Decline and Fall* into his valise as he is starting upon a journey? These great men are not for all hours. But old Howell, and Izaak Walton, and Dick Steele, and Oliver Goldsmith, and Sam Johnson in Boswell, these are of that company of friends to whom we need no critic's introduction. And of this company probably most readers would pronounce Charles Lamb most familiar and most dear.

We may be sure, indeed, that there must have been some unusual power in any personality that can thus transmit its charm through the generations; but we do not care to apply to his work the methods of critical analysis. Moreover, the critic, especially if he be a student of literary evolution, with an itch for explaining things, is likely to find himself put about by Lamb. Because Lamb is not to be accounted for. He doesn't fit into any theory. He doesn't illustrate anything. In describing the course of literary tendencies you don't quite know where to put him. He might as well have lived in the early part of the seventeenth century as in the early part of the nineteenth; in fact, after five o'clock in the afternoon he usually did live in the early part of the seventeenth century. He was fourteen years old when the French Revolution broke out, and the tumult of that movement, with its long reverberations in every department of thought, filled England all his days; but you may read his books and letters without guessing that there ever was a revolution in France — or anywhere else. Some of the intimates of his manhood were very rigid conservatives, like Wordsworth and Southey; one or two were admirers of Napoleon, like Hazlitt; some were extreme doctrinaire revolutionists, like Godwin; but he neither contested their opinions nor adopted them. In himself the elements were so mixed as to make a personality quite unique, not to be classified, and not to be mapped neatly out in an essay.

Doubtless Lamb lives in our imagination chiefly as a humorist. Everybody knows a score of good stories of him, of his whimsicalities of speech and manner, his droll jests, his execrable — and irresistible — puns. We picture him clad in black, like some nervous parson, slipping down Fleet Street of a morning, on fragile legs, — those "immaterial legs," as Tom Hood called them, — to his day's work at the desk in the India House. Getting there a little late, very likely; but, as he said, "I m-make up for that b-by going away early." Or it is on one of those Wednesday evenings in the little room up three flights in the Temple buildings, when the cold ham and ale are on the table, and the door opens to let in Hazlitt, and Godwin, and Procter, and Burney, and Rickman, and Ayrton; and perhaps, on some rare and famed occasion, the heavy form of Coleridge himself comes toiling uncertainly up the stair, and his great forehead, like the dome of Paul's in the babble of London, throws a high dignity over the company. Or, perhaps, one likes best of all to think of him in one of those long evenings at home with Mary, the sister, at one side of the table writing (it may be one of her *Tales from Shakespeare*), and the brother opposite in a halo of smoke — he is certainly going to leave off tobacco next week — reading in some tall folio first edition he has just brought home in triumph, with the feeling of recklessness that follows an extravagant purchase. But wherever he may be, there is, if not always mirth, always humor, and a good humor. His laughter was not like the crackling of thorns under a pot, but genial, kindly, wise. He knew how by a jest, a waggish remark, half drollery and half sympathy, to break up the crust of commonplace that gathers over our thought, to enliven the lead-colored monotony that makes life toilsome and — what is worse — prosaic. And the ability to do this surely is one of the best gifts of genius.

Yet, after all, it is not, I think, his humor that shows most strikingly in Lamb's life, but what, for want of a more precise name, I should call heroism — an undemonstrative, silent, and supremely difficult virtue. In truth, he knows but little of Lamb who cannot discern at the core of his character steadfast resolution, patient endurance. His whole life was a discipline of self-denial and renunciation. From boyhood he was a scholar, with a love for the traditions of learning and the charm of letters. At Christ's Hospital he instinctively selected as his closest

friend that one bluecoat boy who carried better brains
than any other lad of his years in England. Yet
when he left school, in 1792, Lamb could not follow
this friend Coleridge to the University, but, at the age
of sixteen, must begin his lifelong slavery to "the
desk's dull wood." It may have been fortunate for
us that he was thus "defrauded of the sweet food of
academic institution," and forced to that harder
and more varied experience out of which came the
subtle, half-pathetic humor of Elia; but any one who
has read the delightful paper *Oxford in Vacation*
knows how keenly Lamb felt the loss all his days.

Then, in September, 1796, came the solemn tragedy of his life — that black day when there fell upon
his sister Mary the first of those visitations to recur
so often through all her after years, and in sudden
frenzy she took the life of her mother. Lamb gave
up at once all other plans and hopes and loves to
provide for his sister. Nothing could be nobler
than the quiet, self-forgetful temper in which he
accepted that lifelong charge, excusing the selfish
indifference of his elder brother who should have
shared it, and esteeming his exclusive care of Mary
not a burden, but a privilege. He knew that this
duty must set him apart in many ways from his
old friends and associations. That poem, the *Old
Familiar Faces*, surely one of the most pathetic
in our literature, was not written near the close of

his life, but near its beginning, when he was but
twenty-three years old; and recounts the sense of
loneliness and isolation with which he fronted the
coming years: —

"I have had playmates, I have had companions,
   In the days of childhood, in my joyful schooldays,
All, all are gone, the old familiar faces.

*   *   *   *   *   *

"Friend of my bosom, thou more than a brother,
   Why wert thou not born in my father's dwelling?
So might we talk of the old familiar faces —

"How some they have died, and some they have left me,
   And some are taken from me; all are departed;
All, all are gone, the old familiar faces."

We can never know how much that tender and watch-
ful devotion to his sister, through thirty-six years,
cost Charles Lamb. He lived in constant anxiety
for her, fearful now of too much excitement and now
of too much monotony, and always dreading the
oft-recurring summons for their separation. "Don't
say anything, when you write, about our low spirits,"
writes Mary to Sarah Stoddard; "it will vex Charles.
You would laugh, or you would cry, perhaps both,
to see us sit together, looking at each other with long
and rueful faces, and saying, 'How do you do?' and
'How do you do?' and then we fall a-crying and

say we will be better on the morrow. Charles says we are like tooth-ache and his friend gum-boil, which though a kind of ease is an uneasy kind of ease." But it was only to a few of his nearest friends, like Coleridge and Wordsworth, that Lamb would make any mention of his anxieties; and to them almost always in a tone of cheer. Once only, after the repulse of his boyish attachment for Anne Simmons, did he allow himself to think of any other love so near as Mary's — and then only for a few hours. One lonely day in 1819, his long-cherished friendship for that charming actress and large-hearted woman, Fanny Kelly, so far got the better of his prudence that he wrote her a proposal of marriage. When she declined it, with a grace and kindness worthy herself, Lamb sat down at once and wrote the following note : —

" DEAR MISS KELLY, — Your injunctions shall be obeyed to a tittle. I feel myself in a lackadaisical, no-how-ish kind of humor. I believe it is the rain or something. I had thought to have written seriously, but I fancy I succeed best in epistles of mere fun; puns and that nonsense. You will be good friends with us, will you not? Let what has past 'break no bones' between us.

" Yours very truly,

" C. L.

"Do you not observe the delicacy of not signing my full name?

"N.B. Do not paste that last letter of mine into your Book."

Nobody will question the verdict of Lamb's best biographer, Mr. Lucas, that there is no better letter than that in English literature, "nor, in its instant acceptance of defeat, its brave half-smiling admission that yet another dream was shattered, one more pathetic."

Through all those years Lamb never complained; he never railed at the universe; he never put on any airs of heroic endurance or virtuous resignation. He bore his burdens and did his duty like a man. Some of the most characteristic phases of his humor, when closely scanned, turn out to be only the obverse of this manly sincerity and endurance. Just because life was to him so serious a matter, he took delight in upsetting those people who are always mistaking stupidity for seriousness and dulness for dignity. He had perhaps too little patience with those aggressively earnest folk, bent on improving their minds or souls — and ours; especially worthy women of that kind, who have missions and ideas and all that sort of thing. There is a racy letter in which he tells Coleridge of an evening he and his sister have endured tea-drinking with one of Coleridge's admirers, a Miss Benje or Benjay, who discussed Hannah More and Pope's poetry and Doctor Gregory, and defended the opinion that differences of human intellect are the effect of organization. "I attempted to carry it off with a pun on organ, but it went off very flat, and she immediately conceived a very low opinion of my metaphysics, and turning to Mary, put some question to her in French, probably having heard that neither Mary nor I understand French."

So, too, his healthy dislike for all affectations of sensibility often gave a rude shock to the soft sentimentalists. "Mr. Lamb," said a lady to him, "I think so highly of my pastor, because I know him so well; you don't know him, Mr. Lamb, but I know him so well." "N-no, madam," said Lamb, "I d-don't know him; but d-damn him at a venture, madam, d-damn him at a venture!" For himself he had an almost hysterical dread of seeming to invite a condescending sympathy or approval. He refused to be pitied. "For God's sake," he wrote Coleridge, "don't make me ridiculous any more by terming me 'gentle-hearted' in print;" and, in his next letter, "blot out 'gentle-hearted' and substitute drunken-dog, ragged-head, seld-shaven, odd-eyed, stuttering, or any other epithet which truly and properly belongs to the gentleman in question." Genuinely bashful, afraid of being misunderstood, when he deemed his listener either hostile or patronizing, he sometimes took a perverse pleasure in making himself as disagreeable or as inane as possible. It was the contrariness of the boy in him. Patmore said that to those who didn't know him, or knowing, could not or did not appreciate him, he passed for "something between an imbecile, a brute, and a buffoon." One can well imagine his mood when confronted with the grim rigor of Mr. Thomas Carlyle. Yet his most audacious impudence was oftenest put on to cover his own tenderness, or to prevent some over-effusiveness from his friends. "My sister Mary," he said on introducing her to Tom Hood. "Allow me to introduce my sister Mary, she is a very good woman, but she d-drinks!" Underneath all this whimsicality there was a foundation of patient, unselfish endurance. His humor is like his smile; a quizzical yet appealing smile, behind which, they tell us, there always seemed a tender background of far-away sadness — traces of the toil and struggle of his life seen through whatever mask the humor of the hour might put on. "His serious conversation, like his serious writing," says Hazlitt, "is his best. His jests scald like tears, and he probes a question with a play upon words." The heroism of such a life, I should say, is of a higher and harder sort than Mr. Carlyle's loud heroism of eloquence.

There is no need to deny Lamb his frailties. He doubtless exaggerated his own vices, and he took a pleasure in mystifying proper persons by confessing lapses of which he was never guilty; but everybody knows that he was always, in Mary's phrase, rather smoky, and sometimes rather drinky. As he owned, he kept a little on this side of abstemiousness. We may admit, too, that in his last years the resolute, persistent whimsicality of the worn old man was now and then almost painful. He was a little too impatient of the decorum of years; a little too prone to attempt by sheer frivolity to escape the ineluctable demands of age. But he must be either a very blind or a very sour-spirited critic who cannot see that these failings were mostly the result of the tragic circumstance of his life. He was by nature a genial, rather than a jovial, man, select rather than indiscriminate in his friendships. I do not find that in his early years he had any intimate friends besides Coleridge. But after insanity fell upon Mary, he felt himself forced to seek wider and more jovial companionship that he might escape the gloom and monotony of his life, and the danger of such life for her. Some of the acquaintances he picked up while he was slaving for London journals were poor devils like Fell and Fenwick, who could make but slender claim either to ability or to morals; but Lamb, at all events, was attracted by what was best in them, and he never admitted them to the circle of his intimates. He loved the humors of life, and always preferred in his friends some flavor of originality to prosaic common sense. As he says in that acute piece of self-analysis, the Preface to the Second Edition of the *Elia Essays:* —

"He chose his companions for some individuality of character which they manifested. His intimates, to confess a truth, were in the world's eye a ragged regiment. He found them floating on the surface of society; and the color, or something else, in the weed pleased him. The burrs stuck to him — but they were good and loving burrs for all that. He never greatly cared for the society of what are called good people."

George Γ γer, Martin Burney, Jem White, Thomas Manning, William Ayrton — what an interesting company of eccentrics they form; and we should hardly have known them at all had we not met them at Lamb's hospitable bachelor table. And besides them there is a goodly company of friends not unknown to fame, Hazlitt, Procter, Crabb Robinson, Tom Hood, Cowden Clark, Leigh Hunt, and the rest. To say truth, Lamb had a genius for friendship. He could discover something amiable in everybody. He drew about him men who were polar opposites in temperament and bitterly antagonistic in opinion; men like Godwin and Wordsworth,

Hunt and Southey, who would never have given a
hand to each other save on the common ground of
their friendship for Lamb. He stoutly defended them
to each other, and appreciated whatever was genuine
and human in them all. He made free with their
follies, quizzed them on their fads or peculiarities
with an impudence that might have been intolerable
in any one else. " M-martin," he stammered out over
the whist table to Burney, "if d-dirt were trumps,
what a hand you'd hold!" When Coleridge talked
a stricken hour, wrapped in a cloud of lofty meta-
physic, Lamb only remarked dryly, "Coleridge is
so full of his fun!" But no one took offence. Indeed no one could be more quick than Lamb himself to perceive, or more careful to avoid, anything
that might wound the feelings of others. Men who,
like Hazlitt, quarrelled with everybody else, never
could quarrel with him. It was Charles and Mary
Lamb, and one may say only they, that could keep
the friendship of William Hazlitt and Sarah Stoddard,
not only before their ill-assorted marriage, — at
which ceremony Lamb confessed he was convulsed
with mistimed laughter, — but when, in the later
days, they were separated from each other and from
everybody else. Charles and Mary Lamb would
cherish no resentment for any slight, or misunder-
standing, or desertion. When Hazlitt lay in his last
illness alone and unbefriended, it was Lamb who

hastened to visit him, stood by his bedside, and held the hand of the dying man to the end.

But it should be remembered that Lamb's best and closest friends were precisely the best and greatest men of his time. He was surrounded by an oddly assorted company on the Wednesday evenings; but he kept his closest intimacy for two or three — for Coleridge and the Wordsworths. There are few letters in the language like those of Lamb to the Wordsworths, so full of mingled humor and pathos, of the most delicate sympathies. These people really knew each other — which is too uncommon a thing in this world. And this is Lamb's last letter to Coleridge, written probably, as Mr. Dykes Campbell suggests, to remove some mistaken, sick man's fancy: —

"MY DEAR COLERIDGE, — Not one unkind thought has passed in my brain about you. . . . If *you* ever thought an offence, much more wrote it against me, it must have been in the times of Noah, and the great waters swept it away. Mary's most kind love, and maybe a wrong prophet of your bodings! — here she is crying for mere love over your letter. I wring out less, but not sincerer, showers."

Two years later, Coleridge, at the end of his weary illness, turning over the pages of his early poems, comes upon that one, *The Lime-Tree Bower My Prison*, written during the visit of Charles and Mary

Lamb to Nether Stowey, so long ago, when they were all young and happy; and he writes under it: "Ch. and Mary Lamb — dear to my heart, yea, as it were my heart. S. T. C. Æt. 63, 1834. 1797–1834, 37 years!" When he died, Lamb went broken-hearted, murmuring to himself, "Coleridge is dead, Coleridge is dead!" In almost his last recorded lines he writes: "His great and dear spirit haunts me. I cannot make a criticism on men and books without an ineffectual turning and reference to him." And a few days later he followed his old familiar friend. I say it warms the heart to think of such a friendship as this, and makes us deem more nobly of human nature. Thomas Carlyle, seeing Lamb in those last years, notes in him "insuperable proclivity to gin"; judges there is "a most slender fibre of actual worth in that poor Charles." William Wordsworth, writing a few months after Lamb had gone, cries out —

"O he was good, if e'er a good man lived!"

So blindly may the jaundiced cynic misinterpret the man whom the wise poet understands.

II

Literature, it must be remembered, was always an avocation to Lamb. His *Works* were mostly written at the desk's dull wood, where he labored eight —

sometimes nine or ten — hours a day, six days in a week, with only a short vacation in summer, for thirty-six years. In the eighteenth century it used to be thought difficult to be in literature — or in love — and yet attend to business. Pope has some rather mean flings at

> "The clerk foredoomed his father's soul to cross,
>   Who pens a stanza when he should engross."

But in later years it has been found there is neither difficulty nor discredit in such a combination. Lamb is among the first in a long succession of writers — Rogers, Stuart Mill, Anthony Trollope, William Morris, Edmund Gosse, Austin Dobson, Maurice Hewlett, and others — who have managed to unite business and literature without detriment to either. For Lamb, at all events, such a position — save that his hours were too long — was doubtless fortunate. It gave him regular employment which occupied, without overtaxing, his thought; it gave certain and definite remuneration which put him beyond the reach of serious financial anxiety. But a life so confining left not much leisure for literary work; and this may be one reason why, all through his early years, Lamb produced so little. The *Elia Essays*, which to most people stand for Lamb's work, were written after he was forty-five years old; and all his writing before the *Elia Essays* fills only two thin volumes.

But it is not chiefly the confinement of his work at the India House that explains this scantiness of product during the early years; for the *Elia Essays* themselves were mostly written in the years 1820 and 1821, when his duties in the counting room were most onerous.   The truth is, rather, that up to 1820 he had not really found his vein.   His earliest literary aspiration was to be a poet rather than an essayist.   Four sonnets from his pen were included in Coleridge's first volume of verse, published in 1796, and the second edition of that volume, next year, contained a considerable number of short poems by Lamb.   The sonnet form, then for a long time unfamiliar in English verse, he probably borrowed from Bowles, to whose work he had been introduced by Coleridge.   In sentiment, too, by their gentle grace touched with a placid melancholy, these sonnets may remind us of Bowles.   Some fragmentary pieces of blank verse show plainly the influence of Milton and especially of Cowper, whom Lamb in those early days greatly admired. "I could forgive a man for not enjoying Milton," he wrote Coleridge in 1796, "but I would not call that man my friend who should be offended with the divine chit-chat of Cowper."   Burns, also, had been for some years, he declared, the god of his idolatry; but I can see no trace whatever in this early verse of the vigor, passion, or humor of the Scotch poet.

Nearly all the poetry before 1800 came out of the
trials of his own life, the hapless love for the "fair-
haired Anna" and the tragedy of his sister's mad-
ness. Much of it is in a tone of half-despondent
but pious resignation, but with little of Lamb's
peculiar fancy and altogether without humor. It is
all sincere, but only once — in the *Old Familiar
Faces* — do we get the note of sheer intense emotion,
that without the aid of imagery, rhyme, or definite
metre, shapes his lines into truest poetry. The
album verses and the occasional poetry of his later
years are most of them, like the early work, in re-
flective or pathetic, not in humorous, tone. We
recognize frequently in them the quaint fancy of the
seventeenth-century men of whom he was so fond;
in one or two instances the union of subtle or ingenious thought with deep tenderness of feeling makes a
poem of striking quality. Such lines, for instance,
as those he sent to Tom Hood on the death of his
child, *On an Infant dying as soon as Born*, could
hardly have been written by any other poet of the
nineteenth century; to find anything like them you
must go back to Wither or Crashaw. One or two of
the later poems, however, have nothing of this
archaic manner, but, like the *Old Familiar Faces*,
show that unconsciousness of utter sincerity which
is the last charm of lyric verse. The lines to Hester
Savory, the sprightly and comely Quaker girl that

caught his fancy while he was living at Pentonville,

"When maidens such as Hester die,"

once read, can never be forgotten. Lamb had but slender poetic gift, doubtless; yet he wrote two or three lyrics of keen emotional power, and the subtle charm of his personality frequently gave to his more trivial and fragmentary verse an interest which the critic hardly knows how to justify.

Much the same may be said of his early story, *Rosamund Gray*. One might expect, from its plot and its chief actors, this little romance to be a crude mixture of tragedy and sentimentality. The villain is a quite impossible person whom Lamb got out of his reading; he bears the name of one of the murderers in Marlowe's *Edward Second*, and really has no character at all, being a kind of *diabolus ex machina*. Rosamund Gray, the heroine, is one of the helpless, innocent maidens so common in sentimental fiction after Richardson. The action is baldly melodramatic. Yet into this improbable story Lamb has put so much of his native delicacy of feeling, and he has told it with such an artless, old-fashioned grace of style, as to make it altogether delightful, if not altogether convincing. Its opening words strike the note that is sustained throughout:

"It was noon-tide. The sun was very hot. An old gentlewoman sat spinning in a little arbor at the

door of her cottage. She was blind; and her grand-
daughter was reading the Bible to her. The old lady
had just left her work to attend to the story of Ruth."

The *Rosamund Gray*, moreover, has special biographical interest. It was written just after Lamb
had been forced to relinquish thoughts of any
woman's love save his sister's, and it is touched
with the pathos of that resignation. Rosamund
Gray, the mild-eyed maid whom everybody loved,
whose hair fell in bright and circling clusters, is
evidently Lamb's "fair Alice W." More than a
quarter-century afterwards, in that charming essay,
Blakesmoor in H——shire, in describing an old
portrait, he speaks of the bright yellow Hertfordshire hair, "so like my Alice." The lover in the
story, Allen Clare, and his sister Eleanor are Charles
and Mary Lamb; old blind Margaret is their
grandmother, Mrs. Field, whose picture Lamb had
already drawn in one of his early poems; while the
scenery of the tale is that of the home of the fair
Alice, the tiny village of Widmore in Hertfordshire,
which he described so lovingly long afterwards in
the Blakesmoor essay.

A lover of drama and the stage from boyhood, it
was natural that Lamb should try his hand at dramatic composition. But he never succeeded. In
truth, he was without the first requisites of success.

He had little creative imagination, and he had no
constructive ability. He could not conceive or portray original characters; he could not invent effective situations. His farce, *Mr. H.*, which he had
hoped might be a stage success, was promptly
damned before the first representation was half
over — as it deserved to be. Lamb himself, though
chapfallen over his failure, had sense enough to
hiss among the loudest. The motive — the troubles
of a man who endeavors to conceal his name, Hogs-
flesh — is too puerile even for farce; and the changes
are rung on the unfortunate word with dreary repe-
tition. Lamb had not the gift to write a brilliant
or witty dialogue. He could not get out of himself; and his own humor, the humor of Elia, is too
subtle, too peculiarly his own for the broad and
obvious effects that comedy demands. Nor is the
tragedy, *John Woodvil*, much more successful.
It is dignified and serious, and its manner here and
there so close an imitation of the Elizabethans that
Godwin, coming upon some lines from it, was sure
he had seen them in Beaumont and Fletcher. But
it has no real characters, no action, and no adequate
motive for any action. And while the style, in
some passages, may remind us by diction and
rhythm of our elder drama, it has nothing of the
passion and intensity which characterized that large
utterance of the early gods.

In fact, as Mr. Ainger suggests, *John Woodvil* is of interest chiefly as showing how thoroughly Lamb had already immersed himself in our Elizabethan drama. The riper fruits of that study were seen in the volume of *Specimens from English Dramatic Poets*, which appeared in 1808. This well-known book, though it is a florilegium from the older drama with comparatively little comment by Lamb, is probably his most important, as it is his best-known, contribution to literary criticism. We should remember that in 1808 the great body of Elizabethan and Jacobean drama was practically unknown to intelligent readers. Coleridge's lectures did not touch the drama outside of Shakespeare until 1818; Hazlitt's course on the drama was not given until 1821. There were, indeed, some indications of a reviving interest in the drama, as in all our older and romantic literature. Gifford's first edition of Massinger was published in 1805; in 1811, three years after Lamb's book, Weber issued his edition of Ford, warmly commended by Jeffrey in the *Edinburgh*. Yet it may be truthfully said that it was Lamb, rather than any one else, who first led the average well-read Englishman to think he ought to know something of Beaumont and Fletcher, Ford, Massinger, Heywood, Webster. Since his time these old masters have received, perhaps, quite as much praise as they deserve.

97

And for this over-commendation, too, Lamb's book is largely responsible. In truth, whoever forms his estimate of the elder drama from Lamb's specimens will be likely to get an exaggerated idea of its merits. He was captivated by the large imagination in the speech of these men and by their power to show the human soul in its moods of struggle or endurance, beside which the polished conventionalities of later writers seem tame and flat. But his extracts represent their work only at its high points, and give no idea of its crudity and violence, its morbid passion and its frequent distortions of character and motive.

Everywhere, indeed, Lamb's criticism is selective, the criticism of appreciation rather than of impartial estimate. He pays little attention to the meaning and temper of the work as a whole. He does not balance merits and defects; he culls out passages pleasing to linger over with deliberate, prolonged satisfaction. He treated his books as he treated his friends — enjoyed whatever in them was true or original, overlooked or minimized their failings. The rule is perhaps better for friendship than for criticism; yet critical judgment of this sort, if less impartial, is more sympathetic and penetrating. For the same reason Lamb's criticism was not technical or academic, but moral. He cared little for mere form. He brought literature to the test

of life. The author of a book, the characters in a
book, were to him men to be liked or disliked,
to be judged by the same standards we apply
to our neighbors. That is what often makes a
passing remark of Lamb's worth a half-dozen
pages of analysis. Thus, in his rambling essay on
Some of the Old Actors, the few lines in which
he tells how Mrs. Jordan rendered Viola's dis-
guised confession of love show Mrs. Jordan to
have been an excellent actress, but they also reveal
with the utmost delicacy of appreciation the emotion
of Viola. In the same essay is incomparably the
best interpretation of the character of Malvolio
ever written — indeed the only just one that I know
of. These persons were as real to Lamb's thought as
Hazlitt or Manning; he loved to dwell on their
peculiarities, to delight his sense of humor by re-
calling all they say and do. And in every case it
was Shakespeare's Malvolio or Viola that he knew,
not some actor's. An inveterate playgoer, he nevertheless felt the danger of forming acquaintance
with Shakespeare's men and women on the stage
rather than in the study of the imagination. This
is the theme of that essay often thought so paradoxical from him, *On the Tragedies of Shakespeare*. Shakespeare's plays, he declares, are less
suited for representation than almost any other,
simply because there is in his work more of that

element that defies outward expression. In proportion as a play is laden with deep moral significance, in proportion as its inner meaning is more important than its outward action, just in that proportion is the player likely to give it a wrong emphasis. And this is true.

Lamb's critical appreciation was curiously limited. Contemporary works, save those by his personal friends, Coleridge, Wordsworth, and Southey, he seldom looked into. "When a new book comes out," said he, "I read an old one." In those years all the world was reading and praising the poems and novels of Scott; I do not recall any mention of them by Lamb. Byron he detested as a man, and refused to read him — "he is great in so small a way." Shelley's unsubstantial verse he could make nothing of. In truth, he did not much sympathize with any of the new romance. In the Elizabethans romance and adventure were fitting. They lived in an atmosphere of imagination; the world they portrayed was their own world. But that a sober country gentleman who contributed to the *Quarterly Review*, or a dandy lord who was idolized by London society, should go so far afield into mediævalism and orientalism for themes of song or story, that seemed to him labored and unnatural. For himself he liked the homely cockney ways of the town better; and no strange foreign strand had for him

half the charms of that which runs from Charing
Cross to Temple Bar.

Lamb has a few very characteristic papers on the
kindred art of painting.   Perhaps the most ambitious
of all his critical essays is that *On the Genius of
Hogarth*.   He makes no pretension to knowledge of
the artist's technique; he judges a painting solely
by what might be called its literary quality, its imaginative power to suggest vividly some phase of human
life.   Another essay, *On the Barrenness of the Imaginative Faculty in the Productions of Modern Art*,
contains in its few pages more keenness and truth of
vision than are found in many learned modern discussions of realism and idealism.   Contemporary
art, Lamb complains, is content with empty pictorial
effects, and quite powerless to tell anything imagi-
natively.   Not so the elder men.   This essay begins
with a description, or rather an interpretation, of
Titian's great Bacchus and Ariadne in the National
Gallery which makes no mention of Titian's glory of
color, but indicates admirably that wealth of suggestion which seemed to Lamb the secret of art.

" Is there anything in modern art — we will not
demand that it should be equal — but in any way
analogous to what Titian has effected in that wonderful bringing together of two times in the Ariadne in
the National Gallery?   Precipitous, with his reeling

Satyr rout about him, repeopling and reilluming suddenly the waste places, drunk with a new fury beyond the grape, Bacchus, born in fire, firelike flings himself at the Cretan. This is the time present. With this telling of the story an artist, and no ordinary one, might remain richly proud. Guido in his harmonious version of it saw no further. But from the depths of the imaginative spirit Titian has recalled past time, and laid it contributory with the present to one simultaneous effect. With the desert all ringing with the mad cymbals of his followers, made lucid with the presence and new offers of a god, — as if unconscious of Bacchus or but idly casting her eyes as upon some unconcerning pageant — her soul undistracted from Theseus, — Ariadne is still pacing the solitary shore, in as much heart silence and in almost the same local solitude, with which she awoke at daybreak to catch the forlorn last glances of the sail that bore away the Athenian."

Most of Lamb's criticism, however, is fragmentary, informal; much of it is scattered through his private correspondence, especially in the letters to Coleridge, Lloyd, and Wordsworth. There might be culled from his writings a volume of acute and stimulating literary comment. And it should be added that all this early work, whether poetry, story, or criticism, is written in an English chaste, simple, but not meagre, such as hardly any other prose-writer between 1790 and 1810 could command.

But, after all, we shall always think of Lamb not as poet or critic, but as humorist. And rightly. He was, indeed, at the farthest possible remove from that dreary person, the professional humorist. Of all humor his certainly is the most spontaneous and original. He was a species all by himself — a bundle of the most delightful and unaccountable whimsicalities. He had the jester's love for pure nonsense, for the ridiculous, pure and simple. He will suggest with grave face some droll conceit, or tell some waggish story, that trips up the heels of your gravity by its sheer absurdity. Among his minor papers is an account of a fat woman in Oxford, — *The Gentle Giantess*, — that no man who isn't starched intolerably stiff can read without shaking in laughter, — pure farce told in the solemn phrase of Sir Thomas Browne. Of puns, which many people of weighty converse feel bound to depreciate, he was a very great master; and the effect of his puns was doubled, as he very well knew, by his stammer. As one of his friends said, he stammered just enough to make you listen eagerly for the word. His good-natured critical thrusts were often barbed with a pun. "Here's Wordsworth," he stammered, after the poet had been offering some rather lofty criticism on Shakespeare, "he says he could have written *H-Hamlet* himself, if he only had the m-mind!" And then he had a thousand quips and cranks of freakish fancy that altogether defy classification. Of course it was in his talk that these whimsicalities showed best, the suggestions of the moment accompanied by the twinkle of his eye and the droll tones of his speech. Such bubbles burst as soon as blown; they cannot be repeated. Many of Lamb's good things have, indeed, been told over and over again, and deserve to be; yet all who knew him declared that, as we may well believe, no report can give any adequate notion of that talk, — talk like snap-dragon, as Hazlitt said, sparkling with quaint or witty sayings, bits of waggish impudence, happy epithet and allusion, passing abruptly to some large or serious theme, brightened by a constant play of imagination, and shot through with sudden soft lights of tender feeling. It is, I suspect, only in his letters that we get some idea of the charm of his familiar talk. All the letters to Manning, for example, are delectable.

But if the letters give the best picture of Lamb's wit and vivacity, it is in the *Elia Essays* that we see the inmost part of him. There are fifty of these essays. Of this number two are half-humorous fantasies not quite in his best manner, *The New Year's Coming of Age* and *The Child Angel;* seven are critical; eight are papers of humorous observation and comment, like *The Decay of Beggars* or

A Quakers' Meeting; the remaining thirty-four are pure autobiography, concerned entirely with the records of Lamb's own habits, or friendships, or memories. They are all in the first person, and most of them look backward and linger in half-pathetic mood over the charm of things gone by. But in all of them, even in the critical papers, there is a tone of ingenuous confession, a confidence in the sympathy of the reader. There is no ostentation or posing in this, no pride in his interesting self, not a trace of the Byronic temper. Lamb makes a friend of you and tells you what he himself most cares for. Only an honest and kindly nature could venture to unbosom itself so frankly. And even an honest and kindly nature, by presuming too far upon your interest, may easily become a bore; but, though some earnest folk have been known to pronounce Lamb trifling or perverse, it is inconceivable that he should ever be a bore.

Nor is Lamb's humor, at least in the *Elia Essays,* ever idle. His keen enjoyment of the oddities and conceits of life is always tinged with some moral feeling. He delights to quiz our complacent judgments, to look beneath our smug conventions. He is always getting behind some sentimentality, or priggishness, or pedantry, where he can poke delicious fun at it. If he ever grows severe, it is in scorn for those elegant proprieties that too often mask essential coldness of heart. "I shall believe," he says, "in the professions of modern gallantry when in polite circles I see the same attention paid to age as to youth, to homely features as to handsome, to coarse complexions as to clear — to the woman as she is a woman; when Dorimant hands a fish-wife across the kennel or assists the apple woman to pick up her dissipated fruit." On the other hand, he had a liking for all such innocent improprieties, weaknesses, absurdities, as put our human nature at a disadvantage in the eyes of the well-conducted majority. Odd people, unlucky people, tactless people, people in some way left out or left over, though they move his laughter, always appeal to his sympathy. It was not merely in childhood, as he avers, but all through his life, that he had "more yearnings toward that simple architect who built his house upon the sand than for his more cautious neighbor, and prized the simplicity of the five thoughtless virgins beyond the more provident but somewhat unfeminine wariness of their competitors." He might almost have said with Touchstone in the play, "It is a poor humor of mine to take that no one else will." In fact, I have sometimes thought that if you seek the closest parallel to the unique character of Lamb, you will find it, not in any veritable man of letters or history, but in this one of Shakespeare's creations for whom we have no better name than "fool," but who is in

truth one of his wisest and most unselfish men. There
is in both the same curious observation, the same
whimsical liking to turn commonplace wrong side
out, the same quaint fancy, half humorous and half
pathetic, the same fidelity to friends and deep tenderness of heart.

Now it is in the *Elia Essays* that this subtly
humorous temperament finds fullest expression.
Nobody, so far as I know, has succeeded very well
in giving a definition of humor. I certainly shall not
attempt one. But it is one obvious characteristic
of humor that it can find a peculiar pleasure in
the manifold contrasts of life that most of us overlook. When the lofty and the humble are brought
into sudden juxtaposition so as to emphasize
the lofty, then we have the sense of the sublime;
when the contrast emphasizes the humble, then
we have the ludicrous, sometimes with a tone
of irreverence or vulgarity. When suffering or endurance is brought into contrast with the commonplace so as to emphasize the suffering, then we have
the sense of the heroic or the pathetic; when the
commonplace is emphasized, we have the ludicrous,
often of a cynical or unfeeling quality. But there
is a humor which gives us the pleasure of unexpected
contrast without degrading in the least the nobler
element in the comparison, but rather intensifying
it. When Emerson bids us hitch our wagon to a

star, is the saying humorous or sublime? When
Lamb writes to Wordsworth, "God tempers the wind
to the shorn Lambs," is that humorous or pathetic?
In truth it is both; for humor of that sort is fused
with our noblest and deepest feelings. And this is
the humor of which the *Elia Essays* are full; in
every sense a good humor — always reverent, always gentle, humane. As we read these essays, we
feel how oddly patched a stuff is this human life, to
be sure; but its beauties and its virtues seem all the
brighter for the humorous contrast in which they are
set, while our follies and vanities provoke a kindly
laughter because they are thrown up against a background of noble, and serious, and beautiful things.

Obviously, then, such a humor should imply a
quick sensibility for whatsoever things are noble,
and serious, and beautiful. And it does. You
can hardly read a page in these essays without finding proof of that. Now it is a momentary glimpse
of some quiet landscape, usually seen through the
mellowing light of memory, as the Temple gardens,
or the grounds of the old Blakesware mansion, "the
furry wilderness, the haunt of the squirrell and day-
long murmuring wood pigeon, with that antique
image in the centre, god or goddess I knew not."
More often, if it be description, it is of some object
consecrated by long association with the joys and
sorrows of men and calling to our thought some great

complex of experience. For Lamb, though he loved nature well, loved men better. Unlike his friend Wordsworth, who hardly seemed to care for men unless they had somehow passed under the solemnizing influence of mountain and sky, Lamb cared little for nature unless it were somehow humanized — unless, if I may say so, it had been lived in. But he did feel most keenly the charm of all those places or objects about which, for generations, had ebbed and flowed the tides of human life. This was the secret of his love for the town. There any ancient building that thrust its grimy venerableness upon the crowded street might suggest that Elian contrast, half humorous, half sad, between the laughter and loving, the scandal and striving of our little day, and the solemn memory of all the yesterdays. Take, for example, this passage on the sun-dials in the Temple gardens: —

"What an antique air had the now almost effaced sun-dials, with their moral inscriptions, seeming co-evals with that Time which they measured, and to take their revelations of its flight immediately from heaven, holding correspondence with the fountain of light! How would the dark line steal imperceptibly on, watched by the eye of childhood, eager to detect its movement, never catched, nice as an evanescent cloud or the first arrests of sleep!

"'Ah! yet doth beauty like a dial hand
Steal from his figure, and no pace perceived!'

What a dead thing is a clock, with its ponderous embowelments of lead and brass, its pert or solemn dulness of communication, compared with the simple altar-like structure and silent heart-language of the old dials! It stood as the garden god of Christian gardens. Why is it almost everywhere vanished? If its business use be superseded by more elaborate inventions, its moral uses, its beauty, might have pleaded for its continuance. It spoke of moderate labors, of pleasures not protracted after sunset, of temperance, and good hours. It was the primitive clock, the horologe of the first world. Adam could hardly have missed it in Paradise. It was the measure appropriate for sweet plants and flowers to spring by, for the birds to apportion their silver warblings by, for flocks to be led to fold by. The shepherd 'carved it out quaintly in the sun,' and, turning philosopher by the very occupation, provided it with mottoes more touching than tombstones."

What placid grace of rhythm, what quaint felicity of epithet! And what constant play of imagination, suggesting comparisons so unexpected and yet so apt — the movement of the shadow, "nice as an evanescent cloud or the first arrests of sleep!" And how the thought is gently beguiled by hints of sunshine and sweet pastoral toil, to that first garden of all, when the moving shadow began to mark the history of man, and the sun-dial was the "horologe of the first world." And all this poetry is heightened by humorous contrast with the modern clock, "with its ponderous embowelments of lead and brass, and its pert or solemn dulness of communication."

Every one has noticed how rich is Lamb's writing in allusion. His memory was stored with the best things in literature and tradition, — imagery, sentiment, and action, — in the choicest phrase of the masters. All this treasure was at the service of his humor, to illustrate the odd contrast between the threadbare poverty of real life and the boundless wealth of imagination. For in Lamb's allusions the homely commonplace is usually confronted with some fancy, fair or bold; the hard reality with some ideal beauty. The steward who bustles about on the old Margate hoy is like Ariel, "flaming at once about all parts of the deck"; the burly cripple without legs who wheels himself about the streets in a go-cart is "a grand fragment, as good as an Elgin marble"; when the sooty-faced chimney-sweep's grin discloses his double row of white teeth, Lamb quotes: —

> "a sable cloud
> Turns forth her silver lining on the night."

But Lamb's richness of allusion is not best exemplified by images like these, detached from their setting.

It is seen rather in quick turns of humorous phrase, in a single word of quotation, in sudden glimpses and reflections of his reading, so fleeting that we can hardly identify them, yet casting a constant glimmer of humor over the homely facts out of which the essay is woven. In all such allusions the effect is not to degrade the loftier element in the comparison, but to beautify the lower. This is the humor, not of the cynic, but of the poet. It discloses sudden, unforeseen relations between the highest and the humblest things; it makes us feel "how near is grandeur to our dust."

Lamb's literary style is unique. If style be measured by the faithfulness with which it reveals the personality of the writer, then Lamb's must be nearly perfect. To attempt any imitation of it would be to fall into intolerable preciosity. In force and compass, of course, he is not to be ranked with the greatest men; but nobody's work is more exquisite. To use a phrase more commonly applied to painters, I should call Lamb one of the Little Masters. His diction is a study in verbal values. He had a nice sense of the significance of words, the aroma of association. He loved to elaborate a statement slowly, lingering over its details and tasting the flavor of every phrase with deliberate relish. But the charm of his style is due most of all to the constant presence of his imagination. His thought is always concreting itself in illustration or example, and in almost every line blossoms into some rare or graceful fancy. It is so spontaneous that the reader hardly appreciates its richness; but in reality — if the homely phrase may be pardoned — there is more imagination to the square inch in Lamb's writing than in almost any other modern prose.

The archaic cast of his style is due, of course, to the influence of his favorite seventeenth-century men, especially Fuller and Sir Thomas Browne. Not that he slavishly copied these men, or even consciously imitated them; but he had steeped himself in their writing till their manner became second nature. In the preface to the *Last Essays of Elia*, he says, "The essays of the late Elia were villainously pranked in an affected array of antique words and phrases, but they had not been his if they had been other than such; and better it is that a writer should be natural in a self-pleasing quaintness than to affect a naturalness (so-called) that should be strange to him."

In fact, this "self-pleasing quaintness" never does seem affected. Sometimes it gives to a passage an old-fashioned daintiness of manner, as of something laid in lavender: —

"What a place to be in is an old library! It seems as though all the souls of all the writers that have bequeathed their labors to these Bodleians, were reposing here, as in some dormitory, or middle state. I do not want to handle, to profane the leaves, their winding sheets. I could as soon dislodge a shade. I seem to inhale learning, walking amid their foliage; and the odor of their old moth-scented coverings is fragrant as the first bloom of those sciential apples which grew amid the happy orchard."

But more often this seventeenth-century manner serves to emphasize that contrast between the stately and the familiar upon which, as we have said, so much of Lamb's humor depends. As a rule, no form of pleasantry is more inane than the attempt to apply big words to small things. But Lamb's writing seldom degenerates into this form of feeble burlesque. His large utterance seems not only natural to him, but in some way fitting to his theme. There are passages in the essays that, so far as style is concerned, might have been taken bodily out of Sir Thomas Browne's *Religio Medici* or *Urn Burial;* yet their antique dignity of manner seems not misapplied. Take, for example, some sentences from *A Quakers' Meeting :—*

" Dost thou love silence deep as that 'before the winds were made'? go not out into the wilderness, descend not into the profundities of the earth; shut not up thy casements; nor pour wax into the little cells of thy ears, with little-faith'd, self-mistrusting Ulysses. — Retire with me into a Quakers' Meeting.

"For a man to refrain even from good words, and to hold his peace, it is commendable; but for a multitude, it is a great mastery.

"What is the stillness of the desert compared with this place? what the uncommunicating muteness of fishes? — here the goddess reigns and revels. — 'Boreas, and Cesias and Argestes loud,' do not with their interconfounding uproars more augment the brawl — nor the waves of the blown Baltic with their clubbed sounds — than their opposite (Silence her sacred self) is multiplied and rendered more intense by numbers and by sympathy. She too hath her deeps that call unto deeps. Negation itself hath a positive more and less; and closed eyes would seem to obscure the great obscurity of midnight.

"To pace alone in the cloisters or side aisles of some cathedral, time stricken ;

> "'Or under hanging mountains,
> Or by the fall of fountains;'

is but a vulgar luxury compared with that which those enjoy who come together for the purposes of more complete, abstracted solitude. This is the loneliness 'to be felt.' — The Abbey Church of Westminster hath nothing so solemn, so spirit-soothing, as the naked walls and benches of a Quakers' Meeting. Here are no tombs, no inscriptions,

> "'. . . Sands, ignoble things,
> Dropt from the ruined sides of kings' —

but here is something which throws Antiquity herself into the foreground — SILENCE — eldest of things — language of old Night — primitive discourser — to which the insolent decays of mouldering grandeur have but arrived by a violent, and, as we may say, unnatural progression."

In such a passage as this there is far more than the half-humorous adaptation of a stately and antiquated manner. This writing, though so rich with rhetoric that, like some gorgeous stuffs, it will almost stand alone, is cumbered with no idle verbiage. Every epithet is a flash of imagination. That conceit of silence as intensified by numbers is worthy of the subtle Dr. John Donne; and some of the phrases are fairly startling in their vivid boldness. "The insolent decays of mouldering grandeur" — I wonder how many prose-writers of the last two centuries could have hit upon that! To pile together superannuated diction in involved structure is easy enough; but to write a passage like that, in the ampler manner of our elder masters, and yet natural and unstrained, of imagination all compact, informed with grave and quiet feeling and yet played about with lambent lights of humor — this is not easy. Who else besides Lamb in the last century and a half has been able to do anything like it? But then, who has been able to do anything that Lamb did?

For one comes back to the statement that the charm of Lamb's work and character is unique. It eludes analysis. And the better one knows him, the more impossible does it seem to put into words any adequate likeness of the man. His humor, his tenderness, his imagination, his sense of beauty, and his sense of oddity, — they were all peculiar in quality and more subtly combined than in ordinary men.

Only once or twice — perhaps only once, in that most intimate of all his essays, the *Dream Children* — does Lamb drop all affectations and tell us the things that lay nearest his heart in language too utterly sincere even for the disguise of his "self-pleasing quaintness." In that perfect essay humor is quite lost in pathos; and the English in which the simple story is told, for purity of idiom, chaste simplicity, and artless grace of movement, is quite unsurpassed. No one else in Lamb's day wrote such English, and to find anything so perfect you will have to go back to the best passages of the English Bible. Here Lamb has set up a glass where we may see the inmost part of him.

THOMAS DE QUINCEY

I

ONE October afternoon in 1807 a post-chaise was crawling slowly up the long hill that separates the vale of Rydal from the vale of Grasmere in the English Lake District. In the post-chaise sat a lady and her little daughter. Her two boys, of seven and nine, impatient of the slow ascent had alighted, gone on over the brow of the hill, and were briskly running down the other side toward the Grasmere Valley. Behind them followed as fast as he might a short, frail, little man, who looked himself at first glance to be a boy, but whose face, already beginning to be seamed with thought, showed him to be past his first youth. The three had reached the foot of the hill, when a sharp turn in the road suddenly disclosed to their view a little white cottage, roses and jasmine clambering about its windows, and two dark yew trees throwing a protecting shadow over its wall. At sight of this cottage the young man stopped instantly, hesitated, as if about to turn back; but as the boys ran in at the cottage gate, he, too, as if by a sudden impulse of desire that overcame his shyness, pushed in after them. Just at that moment the post-chaise pulled up at the gate, and a tall, grave-looking man with two ladies hurried out from the cottage door to meet it. Our shy but eager young man, who is evidently a stranger to these cottage folk, and for the moment hardly noticed by them, in their haste to greet the lady of the post-chaise, steps modestly into the tiny porch of the cottage and awaits his welcome as the whole party comes in.

This young man, of course, is Thomas De Quincey, travelling to Keswick as an escort for Mrs. Coleridge and her children; he is meeting for the first time, and with trembling reverence, the great Mr. William Wordsworth. A year before he had come up to the Lake District with intent to call upon the poet, and had got a glimpse of the white cottage from the slope of Hammerscar across the lake; but had turned back, afraid to enter the presence of the god of his idolatry. But now he is in the cottage with him, taking tea by his humble fireside, not as with one to be feared, but — to use his own phrase — as with Raphael the affable angel, on the terms of man with man.

This meeting with Wordsworth was a turning-point in the career of Thomas De Quincey. He himself averred that it was marked by a change even in the physical condition of his nervous system. The restless desire, the morbid self-consciousness and self-distrust, the disheartening sense of distance between him and his ideals, — all this vanished in an hour before the homely hospitality of William Wordsworth. It was reassuring to find that the greatest man of the time — for such he thought Wordsworth — was the simplest, content in his retirement among the hills, and careless of the loud noises of fame. But whatever influence this meeting may have had upon the mental development of De Quincey, it certainly may be considered as the beginning of a new period in the outward history of his life. Up to this time he has been a sort of vagrant, without fixed place of residence, without any definite purpose, without any congenial friends. Coleridge he had met a few weeks before this visit to Grasmere; now he has met Wordsworth; three days later he is to meet Southey; a few months later he will meet John Wilson. These men, in spite of differences and temporary estrangements inevitable with such a temperament as his, remained his best, almost his only, friends for more than half his lifetime. The next summer he visited Wordsworth again; and when, in 1809, Wordsworth left this little cottage, he took it, and called it his home for more than twenty years. Hither, after some six years of bachelor life, he brought a wife from a farmhouse at Rydal Water a mile away; here his children were born. It is hardly too much to say that the direction of all his later life was determined by this visit to Wordsworth.

It is not easy, however, to trace with accuracy his doings or his whereabouts, either before or after that event. Some early passages in his life he himself described with great detail in those sketches afterwards pieced together for the Autobiography. But the Autobiography is no connected narrative. It is rather a series of pictures of some moments in which the life of long periods seemed focussed, incidents in which his personality was revealed to himself, or the sadness and wonder of the world struck in upon his soul. The incidents, moreover, are related as they stood in his memory years after they occurred, when his morbidly heightened fancy had doubtless enveloped them with circumstance unnoticed at the time or altogether imaginary. When all his life had passed into the atmosphere of dream, he never could quite tell how much of it was fact and how much was only dream.

The one significant fact that seems clear from these records is that De Quincey and all his brothers and sisters were precocious young folk, with a certain wayward intensity of imagination. Two of his sisters died in early childhood, both from some affection of the brain. His eldest brother, who died in young manhood, was a singularly brilliant boy, who lived for years most of the time in a realm of romance of his own creation, and had strength of will enough to make his brothers live there, too. The younger brother, Pink, ran away to sea in his teens, was captured by pirates, recaptured, served in the navy, and in a dozen years passed through a series of adventures wild enough for a Stevenson romance. Whence they got this strain in their blood it might be hard to say; for their father was a well-to-do merchant of Manchester, prosaic enough, for all that appears, both in character and pursuits. Thomas De Quincey at thirteen years of age, — if we may take his word for it, — could read Greek with ease, and at fifteen not only wrote lyric Greek verse, but conversed in Greek fluently, and was in the habit of reading off the daily newspaper into that language — a process that must have racked the Greek considerably. "That boy," said one of his masters, "could harangue an Athenian mob better than you or I could address an English one." His father had died when De Quincey was only seven years of age, and the boy was kept in school by his guardians, under an uncongenial master, after he should have been at the University. He ran away, and as he flatly refused to go back, his mother gave him a guinea a week and let him wander wherever he would. He drifted about for some months in Wales, living in farmhouses, and astonishing the good folk by his courtesy and his erudition; and towards winter made

his way up to London. His adventures here: how
he slept starving and shivering in a Greek Street
garret, how he roamed the city with Anne of Oxford
Street and fainted of cold and hunger in Soho Square,
how he was helped by the good Jews at the rate of
eighteen per cent, and at last by some fortunate
accident — he never told what — he was discovered,
restored to his friends, and sent up to Oxford where
he belonged, — all this will be remembered by everybody, for everybody has read the *Confessions*. Yet
the story raises some doubts. Without question it is
true in outline; but I think it must be embroidered a
little. This romantic tramping in Wales with his
mother's consent and a guinea a week; all this
vagabondage and starvation in London when there
was bread enough and to spare in his mother's house,
— it seems too much to believe of a rational mother
or a rational son. I suspect the laudanum has got
into the story.

He entered Worcester College, Oxford, in 1803,
and he was there through 1808; but he couldn't
have kept his terms regularly in the latter year, and
seems not to have been in residence much after the
summer of 1807. He formed no intimacies in
college, lived much by himself, and as, from some
freak or other, he refused to stand his final examina-
tions, he never took a degree. But he seems to have
read a good deal in literature and philosophy; and

he was one of the few young men who hailed with genuine appreciation the early work of Coleridge and Wordsworth.

In 1809 he took up his residence in the Lake District, occupying the little Grasmere cottage that Wordsworth was then vacating; but what he was doing there for the next twelve years nobody knows. He had adopted no profession. He wrote no books or reviews, and seemed to have no clear vocation to literature. No one knew or saw much of him. He says himself that he was reading German metaphysics and taking opium. Both habits he had acquired while in the University; both accorded well with his dreamy, isolated temper; both he kept up during life. In 1819, urged by the needs of an increasing family, he became editor of a local newspaper in Kendal; German metaphysics and Tory politics, however, made a mixture not relished by his rural readers, and after some months he gave up that project. But two years later, in 1821, appeared in the *London Magazine* the *Confessions of an Opium-Eater*, and De Quincey's literary career was begun. For the next four years he was much in London, preparing for the *London Magazine* a series of some dozen papers continuing and supplementing the *Confessions*. By 1826 he got the ear of the public and was a coveted contributor.

After about this time, however, his interests drew

him away from London to Edinburgh. For more than ten years his closest friend among his neighbors in the Lake District had been, not Wordsworth, for whom his early reverence had now somewhat abated, but John Wilson of Elleray. Wilson was now at the height of his popularity as editor of *Blackwood's Magazine*, and had already once or twice ventured to introduce the *Opium-Eater* as a character into his famous *Noctes Ambrosianae*. He now persuaded his friend to lend his pen to the service of *Blackwood*, and after 1826 De Quincey became a frequent contributor to that brilliant periodical. In 1834 *Tait's Magazine* was set up in Edinburgh; it was for these two journals, *Blackwood* and *Tait*, that most of De Quincey's work was done for the rest of his life. In 1830 he removed his family to lodgings in Edinburgh; and in 1837, after the death of his wife, took a cottage at Lasswade, a little way out of the city, which was his home — or at all events the home of his children — so long as he lived. For himself he preferred to do his writing in hired rooms in town, near his publishers; and it is part of the De Quincey legend that he used to occupy a room until it was entirely "snowed up" with papers and manuscripts which he despaired of arranging and yet would not destroy, when he would back out and hire another room, only to be pushed out of this again by the ever accumulating mass of papers.

What seems certain is that he must have produced a vastly greater amount of manuscript than he ever got printed; had he published all he wrote, the array of his works might have been something appalling. In his later days he was one of the celebrities of Edinburgh; but it was difficult to get sight of him; for he refused most of the conventions of society and usually had to be found, if found at all, buried in some of his bookish retreats. He kept on writing to the end; but the last years of his life were mostly spent in garnering up his scattered papers from the magazines, revising and arranging them for a collected edition of his works. In spite of the ill-health by which he had always been harassed, in spite of his life-long opium habit, — or possibly because of it, — the fragile little man outlived all his early friends, and died in 1859, at the good old age of seventy-four.

II

After all no one seems to know much of De Quincey; no one ever did know much of him. When you have read all his own *Confessions*, you feel he has told you little of himself, of his pursuits, his practical outward life, still less of his affections, his inner life. A very considerable body of reminiscence from his contemporaries has, indeed, gathered about his memory, and some thirty years ago Mr. Japp —

or, as for some unknown reason he preferred to call himself, Mr. Page — wrote his life in two stout volumes; yet all the letters and the stories leave us with the feeling that we have not really got inside that strange personality. The truth is there seems something demonic, almost spectral, about De Quincey. He wasn't one of your men of large red health, who stand solidly on the ground, and love the broad plain facts of life. He lived in the Grasmere cottage twenty years; but he formed few acquaintances and left few memories there. Of all his Grasmere neighbors, Dorothy Wordsworth, who had that gift for appreciating genius which is itself a form of genius, always understood him best, and her sympathy and judgment several times stood him in good stead. People of plain common sense naturally found him difficult. Harriet Martineau, — a very large incarnation of common sense, — who lived near him for years, declared that his absorption and selfish moodiness had rendered him quite insensible to the ordinary requisites of honor and courtesy, to say nothing of gratitude and sincerity. But Harriet Martineau was herself rather difficult. In those years of the Grasmere residence he was generally invisible; for he preferred to read and dream indoors by day, and come forth to walk by night. Many a night, past midnight, when all the valley was hushed in slumber and lights had ceased to twinkle in the cottages, his little form might have been made out, flitting like some darker shadow up the hillside, over the fells, or resting in some secluded nook by the Rothay.

Neither in his own house or anywhere else did the ordinary conventions of society ever get much hold on him. At the call of some chance thought, his daughter says, he might interrupt the process of dressing himself in the morning, and forget altogether to resume it, perhaps receiving a visitor later in the day without his coat or wearing half the proper number of stockings. Going to call on Professor Wilson in Gloucester Place, Edinburgh, one stormy evening, he decided to remain over night, and literally stayed a year. During all this visit, Wilson says, he lived in a kind of mysterious seclusion, spending most of his days locked in his room, stretched on the floor before the fire, and was only seen when toward midnight he stole out of doors for a long walk. If he could be captured at a late dinner lasting till two or three in the morning, he would sometimes pour forth a stream of talk that entranced all his hearers. As a rule, however, he refused to take his meals with others; and Wilson's servants used to place food outside the door of his room, leaving him to take it when he liked, and often finding it twelve hours later untouched. Later on, in 1843, Wilson declared that, though he supposed himself to be the most intimate friend of De Quincey, and the De Quincey family, then living at Lasswade, frequently sent to him for news of their father, yet he had seen him not above four times in six years. Even his own family, it is clear, always deemed him an odd creature.

This peculiar abstracted temper was aggravated, doubtless, by the opium habit; but it was not engendered by opium. De Quincey was born with eyes that open inwards. He lived in a world of his own — a world of dream and speculation. Not that he was altogether without interest in outward affairs, social, economic, or political; but he was unable to take the obvious and practical view of them. With an almost preternatural gift to discover subtlety or paradox, he was as helpless as a child before the simplest business difficulty. He wandered half over Edinburgh one evening trying to negotiate a personal loan for seven shillings sixpence, and offering as security a fifty-pound bank-note; at the same time he was writing a treatise on the *Logic of the Laws of Wealth*. In this isolation and self-absorption there was nothing of cynicism or misanthropy. On the contrary, there often seemed to be in his manner a kind of timid appeal for human sympathy and companionship. He left upon you the impression of a man "moving about

in worlds not realized." He had a soft and dep-
recating tone in his voice and a gentle but elaborate
courtesy which he extended to everybody alike.
Professor Wilson's daughter says that when he was
staying in their house, he would inform the cook with
a stately deference, as if he had taken her for a
duchess, that "owing to dyspepsia affecting my
system, and the possibility of any additional derangement of the stomach taking place, consequences
incalculably distressing would arise, so much so
indeed as to increase nervous irritation, and prevent me from attending to matters of overwhelm-
ing importance, if you do not remember to cut
the mutton in a diagonal rather than in a longitu-
dinal form."

But with a friend, or even with a comparative
stranger whom he had reason to think thoroughly
sympathetic, De Quincey could come out of his withdrawn and silent mood, and be a most delightful
companion. No subject could be started in conversation that would not soon touch some topic in
which he felt an interest; then a flush would spread
itself over the withered little face, the eyelids would
lift, slowly and as with an effort, disclosing a pair of
wonderful, immortal eyes, the feeble mouth would
tremble and twitch for an instant, and then his talk
would begin. Low-voiced, deliberate, as if far away,
eddying hither and thither, circling about all sorts

of topics yet never quite losing its way, monotonous
in tone always, but in matter varied, brilliant, eloquent, full of ingenious reflection, curious fact,
striking paradox, flavored with bits of caustic satire
or gossip, shot through with strange lights of fancy.
"What wouldn't one give," said Mrs. Carlyle, when
first she saw him in an evening company, "what
wouldn't one give to have that little man in a box
and take him out now and then to talk?" Everybody that ever met him intimately, — Tom Hood,
Professor Wilson, Harriet Martineau, Hill Burton,
Professor Masson, Mr. Fields, Mr. Gillies, and half
a score of other people, — they all testify to that
marvellous stream of talk. But, curious to say, so
far as I can discover, not one of them ever remembered a dozen words of what he said. They descant
upon the fluency, the music, the subtlety, the learning of his talk; but what, on any given occasion,
Mr. De Quincey was actually talking about, nobody
seems to have recorded. In truth it probably didn't
much matter. Evidently it was the extraordinary
brilliancy of the exercise that fascinated his hearers,
rather than any definite body of opinion. It wasn't
talk like Johnson's, made up of stout, well-shaped
propositions to be defended against all disputants,
but rather a winding stream of speculation and rhetoric, sweeping its long curves through the borders
of a dim land of dreams.

III

Now all of De Quincey's literary work is just this talk put into print. He wrote easily — too easily; it was his mode of talking to himself, and those mounds of manuscript that filled, one after another, the dens in Edinburgh where he spent his days were only other masses of talk that did not get into print. As you open his book you hear the man going on with his monologue. There on the printed page is the curious combination of volubility and precision, the garrulity, the discursiveness, the love of paradox, the indifference to the obvious and the vision for the remote, the labored humor, — all those qualities that, they tell us, used to mark his conversation. Of him it may be said in a very special sense that he being dead yet speaketh. And herein is the best assurance for the permanence of his work. Any writing that can preserve for us in such vivid completeness the personality of a man is sure to live; certainly if that personality be so interesting as De Quincey's.

On the other hand, writing like this has some very obvious and very serious defects; so serious as to make it doubtful whether most of De Quincey's work can ever rank very high as literature. The truth is that talk, however wonderful, is not exactly literature; it needs first to be composed. But De Quincey never really composed anything. There is no method in his work, no clear foresight of the end from the beginning, nothing final and finished. With all his learning and subtlety he never wrote anything to be properly called a treatise, though he planned several. His essays, critical or historical, are full of curious fact and conjecture, personal speculation and personal reminiscence, ranging from Dan to Beersheba, but they are seldom or never the clear, well-arranged presentation of the subjects they profess to discuss. He gives a variety of incidental suggestion, frequent illuminating glimpses of the recondite relations of his theme; but he fails in the humbler, though more important, task of giving to his subject ordered and unified treatment. In fact, he never was a direct or systematic thinker. His mental habits were so discursive that, although he had great penetration, he was nevertheless always something of the dilettante. The most miscellaneous of writers, in his last days he was sorely put to it to make any intelligible plan of arrangement for his collected work; and his latest editor has broken up that plan without being able to devise any much better. A sort of Admirable Crichton, he did nothing with his knowledge, he reached no conclusions, he settled no questions, marked out no new paths for human thought; and the large familiar elements of life out of which great literature is made, man's love and hope and desire, — still less to these could he give such expression as shall thrill or inspire. He could only gossip; curious, usually interesting, sometimes instructive, it was still gossip — gossip through fourteen stricken volumes.

But this is not the worst. Gossip is often delightful. But this talk, page after page, in the cold print, without the fascinating voice and presence of the Opium-Eater himself, if I mistake not, will often try the patience of the reader. We find ourselves remembering that life is short. De Quincey is excellent reading, if you have leisure; but of leisure he demands a great deal. Professor Masson suggests that a young man could do no better than to take three months and read through the whole body of De Quincey's writing. Such a course would doubtless sharpen his intellect and broaden greatly the range of his knowledge; but I suspect the young man would have some heavy half-hours. Yet another critic, Mr. Saintsbury, remarks it is probably in youth that the merits of De Quincey are best appreciated; he ought to be read, thinks Mr. Saintsbury, when you are about fifteen or sixteen. Much of De Quincey would probably tax the brains of a lad of sixteen; yet Mr. Saintsbury may be right in deeming that age most tolerant of De Quincey's manner. For at sixteen there seems time enough for anything; art is short and life is long; before we are fifty we learn better.

We admit to those who admire his style that De Quincey is never verbose; he never repeats the same thought with needless fulness of phrase. But he is the most prolix of mortals. Tennyson says of the flower in the crannied wall —

> "I pluck you out of the crannies,
> I hold you here, root and all, in my hand,
> Little flower — but if I could understand
> What you are, root and all, and all in all,
> I should know what God and man is."

It is this kind of knowledge of every fact and every truth that De Quincey seems bent on imparting. In a very suggestive passage of the *Reminiscences* he says that in early youth he labored under a peculiar embarrassment whenever he sought to convey his thought in language: "It was not words only I wanted; but I could not unravel, I could not even make perfectly conscious to myself, the subsidiary thoughts into which one leading thought often radiates; or, at least, I could not do this with anything like the rapidity requisite for conversation. I labored like a sibyl instinct with the burden of prophetic woe as often as I found myself dealing with any topic in which the understanding combined with deep feelings to suggest mixed and tangled thoughts; and thus partly — partly also from my invincible habit of revery — I had a most distinguished talent 'pour le silence.'" This states admirably the mode of thought he coveted when young, and attained in such perfection in his maturer years. With a marvellous richness of vocabulary and the utmost precision of phrase, he was never content to isolate a truth from its connections, as it is needful to do if we would give a clear statement of it in moderate compass. He must pull his thought up by the roots, and then trace out with laborious precision all its minute filaments, and its ramifications into a network of other thought. Everything reminds him of something else. Now if he had, and we had, the secular leisures of a Methuselah, this would be a most profitable exercise; but the result in our little day is that he exhausts our patience and doesn't exhaust anything else.

In the treatment of any subject De Quincey seldom begins at the beginning; he begins a good way back of the beginning. He has to work inward through a thicket of secondary suggestion that has grown up about his original thought, and his path is sure to be circuitous and broken by numerous side excursions. Take as an example his method of approach to the leading proposition of one section of his famous essay on *Style* — the proposition that Greek literature is concentrated in two periods about seventy-five years apart. That is a simple historical statement, and one would think it might be laid down and proved at once. How does De Quincey get at

it? He begins with a reference to the late Latin
poet, Velleius Paterculus, and proceeds to give a
sketch of his life and times in three pages; then comes
the statement for which Paterculus was called in,
to the effect that genius tends to "agglomerate";
the passage is given in the original, and translated
clause by clause, with an embroidery of discussion
on the style of Paterculus — three pages more; then
come examples from various literatures ancient and
modern, proving the truth of the assertion of Paterculus — four pages more; then the reasons in the
constitution of the human mind for this periodic
manifestation of genius, and the consequent necessity
of the alternation of creative and critical periods —
four pages more; and then, at last, we come to our
central proposition that there were two such periods
in Greek literature. All this preliminary pother over
Paterculus is quite needless; it does not prove or
really introduce De Quincey's main thesis; it is all
excrescence.

Sometimes he is quite unable to get through this
preliminary matter, and never reaches his central
theme at all. Like Coleridge, he has the exasperating trick of promising some elaborate discussion or
exposition, bringing up horse, foot, and dragoons to
make ready, and then abruptly retiring from the
field. All readers of Coleridge's *Biographia Literaria* will remember the lively anticipation with

which they — unless forewarned — expected his promised discussion of the *Imagination or Esemplastic Faculty;* and the inclination to profanity when they found Coleridge suddenly deciding, after all his parade of preparation, to postpone the discussion to some more convenient season. De Quincey, in his *Letters to a Young Man,* does precisely the same thing with reference to the philosophy of Kant. He informs his correspondent that he will do what divers other philosophers have vainly essayed to do, give him a succinct statement of the fundamental positions of the Kantian philosophy. Ah, thinks the reader, now we have something definite and much to be desired. But, first, De Quincey must expose the ignorance and folly of previous expositors — six of them; then he must remind his correspondent that the difficulty of Kant arises principally from his terminology, and show that a new terminology is a necessity in a new philosophy. By that time he is at the end of his sheet, and forced to postpone the exposition of Kant to another letter — which he never wrote.

And even when he does reach his theme, his treatment of it is often sadly lacking in proportion. Some of his critical essays, for example, are so largely taken up with subordinate or collateral matters as to give you little help in estimating the essential character or value of the work criticised. You have been amused with a great variety of minor considerations, but you come out at the end a little mazed, asking yourself what you have got, after all; and as far as the main object of your search is concerned, very much in the condition — if I may borrow one of De Quincey's own jokes — of the student to whom was propounded the old Cambridge problem, "Given the captain's name and the year of our Lord, to determine the longitude of the ship."

Perhaps it is in his narrative writing that we find the most remarkable instances of this vagabond manner. It is true, indeed, that here it usually doesn't so much matter. When De Quincey is recounting his own experiences, his rambling garrulity is rather pleasant. We know he will never get through; this is no story to be finished. When he has talked long enough he will stop; and we need listen no longer than we wish. I don't know that any special illumination is spread over De Quincey's life in the Manchester Grammar School by telling us that his mother had a friend who, when a pretty widow of thirty-six, had married an ugly German named Schreiber, who took snuff; that Mrs. Schreiber, afterward separated from Schreiber, took charge of two orphan girls from India, and placed them under a system of excellent discipline that it takes fifteen pages to describe; that one of these girls, with a Madonna-like face and almond-shaped eyes, married

Lord Carberry, studied New Testament Greek with
De Quincey, and discussed with him for ten pages the
relation of the Christian religion to pagan morality;
that Mrs. Schreiber, having a cancerous affection,
called in the services of a distinguished surgeon, Dr.
White, who administered hemlock with some bene-
ficial effects; that Dr. White's two daughters were
very fond of Lady Carberry — especially the younger;
that Dr. White had a museum and in it a mummy and
a skeleton; that the mummy was deposited in a tall
clock case, the face covered with a piece of white
velvet and not disclosed even to Lady Carberry;
that some seventy years before, when there was still
something of glamour about the life of the highway-
man (for which plausible reasons may be adduced in
three pages) there had been a notable robbery and
murder committed in a brick house on the west side
of the college green in the city of Bristol, near where
Southey and Coleridge afterward lived, and forty-
eight hours before the robbery, a very tall, handsome
young man, respected by his neighbors, had ridden
out of the village of Knutsford, and was by many
suspected to have been the robber; and that the
skeleton in the museum of Dr. White, who attended
Mrs. Schreiber, who reared Lady Carberry, who
talked Greek with De Quincey, *may* have been the
skeleton of this robber. All this isn't exactly necessary to our conception of the life and studies of young

De Quincey in the Manchester Grammar School, but it is amusing. To be sure, a life of De Quincey written on this plan would reach "from here to Mesopotamy, a thing the imagination boggles at"; but De Quincey isn't writing his life, he is only talking.

In argument or exposition, where we have a right to expect method and conclusion, this manner is less excusable. Yet here it is not due to revery or mere vagrancy of thought, but rather to De Quincey's irresistible tendency to chase every subject into all its relations. He himself justly claimed to be a vigorous and accurate thinker; but his mind was fascinated by the complexity of forces that enter into every event, the tangled skein of motives that issue in every volition. Minds of this habit cannot contemplate one thing at a time, and so are ill-fitted for clear exposition; they cannot decide promptly, and so are ill-fitted for efficient action. But they often greatly stimulate and broaden other minds. They disclose unsuspected truth, and show the profounder reason that underlies our conventional beliefs. Coleridge is an excellent case in point; in imaginative literature the familiar example is *Hamlet*. If De Quincey has left us nothing of high philosophic worth, this is not so much because his intellect was less acute than that of Coleridge or even because he had less power of concentration; but rather because he could never bring himself to observe any just proportion or relative value among the subjects of his thought. He will often overlook all the obvious and important phases of his theme to trace out some remote or unfamiliar implication. He seems to care more for novelty than for truth, and is more interested to surprise than to persuade. Nothing pleases him better than to fasten to some familiar proposition a long sorites, and then follow his sorites underground till the conclusion emerges at last in some quite unexpected quarter. He loves thus to disclose links of cause we had never thought of, or show the inadequacy of some generally accepted notion. For example, the great literature of Greece, he says, owes many of its distinctive qualities to the fact that it never could be, in the modern sense of the word, published. But why was it not published? Why, of course, you say, because the art of printing had not then been invented. Oh, no, rejoins De Quincey, that is not the reason; that is a foolish reply; the art of printing had been invented and lost again half a dozen times before the fifteenth century — witness the beautiful inscriptions upon coins. It was not printing that was lacking, but paper. And why paper? Because there were no cotton or linen rags. And why no rags? Because people almost universally wore woollen clothing. And thus the fact that the Greeks wore woollen clothes determines the literary style of their writing.

The humor of De Quincey, when it is genuine and spontaneous, usually proceeds from this same liking to trace remote or unexpected affiliations of thought. Much of his humor, however, is neither genuine nor spontaneous. I must confess I cannot find much humor in the famous paper on *Murder as a Fine Art*. The phrase that forms the title is witty, and had it been used in conversation to point a satiric reference, might have been a brilliant *bon mot;* but to work the subject out, with laborious ingenuity into all its grewsome details, preserving the while the temper of the connoisseur, this is merely a forcible inversion of our normal feeling. It is hardly to be called humor at all; certainly it is not a good humor. Nor is there any purpose in it; there is no irony in the paper, no satiric intent, no truth of any sort under the fooling. De Quincey pleaded the example of Swift in some of his grim jesting in Gulliver, or the famous "Proposal" for eating the children in Ireland. But there is no real similarity in the cases. Swift's papers are examples of the most awful satire; Swift is in sad and terrible earnest. Similarly De Quincey might, one thinks, have written a satire, for example, upon the tendency of a certain school of dramatists to treat the seventh commandment as he had treated the sixth; but he did not. He was aiming only to be facetious; and neither Adultery nor Murder as a Fine Art is matter for pure comedy. Another very

dreary form of De Quincey's attempts at humor is
his heavy jocularity and vulgar slang, a sort of labored gaucherie.   Throughout a long essay he calls
the historian Josephus "Wicked Joseph," or "Mr.
Joe"; he tells at great length, in another essay, the
story of Bentley's famous lawsuit with Colbraith —
whom he terms a "malicious old toad" — and at the
end, or, as he puts it, "when the last round is over,"
he calls out: "Well, Colbraith, how do you find yourself by this time?   I think you'll not meddle with our
Dick again" — our Dick being, of course, the great
Richard Bentley.   After quoting a passage from
Cicero, he goes on, "After such a statement as this
did Kikero not tumble downstairs and break three of
his legs in his haste to call a public meeting?"   When
he can no longer contain his astonishment or indignation, he will occasionally relieve himself, not by
a good round "damn" — which would at least be
spontaneous — but by some such elegant expletive
as "O crimini!"   This sort of thing from a man
of culture is certainly surprising; but most readers
will not deem it witty.   He can now and then be
sprightly and diverting without descending to this
horse play, as, for example, in his banter upon Coleridge's two friends, Ball and Bell — Sir Alexander
Ball who had no abstract ideas, and Dr. Andrew
Bell who had two, one on the moon and the other on
education.   Yet even in such raillery he is never quite

safe from some slip into vulgarity. His deliberate attempts at the facetious are always likely to be forced. His best humor seems quite unconscious, some form of that waywardness and whimsicality characteristic of his thinking. Mr. Bagehot says somewhere that there is humor in the thought of an immortal soul tying his shoe-string. It is this contrast between the infinite and the trivial, the strange immanence of the sublime in the commonplace, that fascinates De Quincey, and occasionally issues in passages of peculiar and genuine humor.

But this sense of the infinite significance and suggestion in common things is best seen in De Quincey's many passages of pathos or sublimity. His imagination had power to interpret the wide possibilities latent in the present and the actual. He can trace with marvellous skill the subtle links of thought or feeling by which the simple incident, the passing emotion, may draw into the study of our imagination a vast complex of experience, with all its contrasts of good and evil, of joy and sorrow. Thus while on a visit to Windsor he watches a group of young men and women in a contra-dance. This suggests to him, first, a protest against that tendency in all the arts to substitute the difficult for the beautiful which had almost pushed out of use this graceful, old-fashioned dance; then comes a discussion — relegated to a page-long footnote — of the disputed etymology of the term "contra-dance"; after this he gives a brief but subtle analysis of the emotion of "passionate sadness" evoked by the spectacle of the dance, and an explanation of the fact that all our highest and most festal emotions are tinged with melancholy; and then, at last, in a passage of lofty rhetoric and solemn music he renders the large imaginative significance of the scene with its vague power over our emotions: —

"A sort of mask of human life, with its whole equipage of pomps and glories, its luxury of sight and sound, its hours of golden youth, and the interminable revolution of ages hurrying after ages, and one generation treading upon the flying footsteps of another; whilst all the while the overruling music attempers the mind to the spectacle, the subject to the object, the beholder to the vision."

Any ordinary experience may suffice thus to set his imagination at work, and produce one of those purple patches that, everybody knows, are scattered so thickly though his pages.

Closely akin to this feeling of indefinite emotional meanings inherent in common things was De Quincey's liking for mystery of every sort. He was used to say he could not live without it. He relished any tale of wonder, dreams, omens, popular superstitions, any mere cock-and-bull story. He wrote papers on

Free Masonry, On the Order of the Rosy Cross, on the *Pagan Oracles*. The opening lines of Macbeth — the creepy chant of the witches — haunted him all his days; and his paper on the *Knocking Scene*, altogether apart from the characteristic subtlety of its reasoning, shows what a shudder that eerie bit of stage business gave to his imagination. But he had, at the opposite extreme of sensibility, a deep, half-mournful awe before the inscrutable mystery in which our lives are rooted. Always restless within the narrow limits of positive knowledge, he loved to send his thoughts out beyond those confines into that dim border-land of imagination and conjecture where knowledge shades into wonder and loses itself in the dark profound. He had little of Wordsworth's interest in the common face of nature, but at times some sight or sound would lay sudden awe upon him — as that summer wind which began to blow while he stood by the corpse of his sister, hollow, solemn, Memnonian, as if it had swept the fields of mortality for centuries, the one audible symbol of eternity! All his readers will remember passages of speculation in which De Quincey is lifted into sublimity by his solemn sense of the infinity of all our human powers and affections. Like Sir Thomas Browne, whom he so much admired, he loved to pose his apprehension with mysteries, and pursue his reason to an *O altitudo!*

After going over the whole body of De Quincey's
Works, one is constrained to admit they contain
rather surprisingly little of substantive and permanent value. The most industrious of writers, his
energy was dissipated upon a multitude of curious
topics, and he never finished, or even attempted, any
work of signal importance. Of the practical, outward life of men, such a shy and secluded bookworm
could have no real knowledge. He has really nothing to say upon all the urgent political and social
questions that were agitating the minds of Englishmen all his lifetime. You will get no aid from him
for the conduct of life. He lived in his own quiet
world of books, of dreams, of memories.

This statement suggests what is perhaps the simplest and best classification of his writings. With
unimportant exceptions they fall into three groups,
as they are concerned with his reading, his imagination, or his personal reminiscences. In the first of
these groups would be placed his papers on literary
biography and history, on literary theory, and the
purely critical appreciations of individual writers.
The biographical sketches, like those of Shakespeare,
Pope, Bentley, are always interesting, but they lack
proportion. De Quincey cared little for the plain,
outward facts that make up the greater part of
every man's life, and was constantly drawn away to
the more curious but less important phases of char-

acter and action. Or, if his subject be one inviting epic treatment, like Joan of Arc, he may omit all historical detail and lift his essay into a kind of ode or heroic declamation. His more characteristic historical papers, however, are usually concerned with some of the enigmas or curiosities of history, *The Essenes, The Pagan Oracles, The Character of Cicero, The Casuistry of Roman Meals, Judas Iscariot*. But of the papers in this first group, the most valuable are not biographical or historical. Knowing far more of literature than of life, always interested in questions of rhetorical form, it was natural that De Quincey should put some of his best thinking into the essays on literary theory. He has perhaps nowhere written anything more thoughtful and fertile than the *Letters to a Young Man*, and the essays on *Rhetoric, Style,* and *Conversation*. These papers do not, indeed, make any systematic body of critical philosophy, but they abound in detached statements of principle, always penetrating, and sometimes — like the distinction between the literature of knowledge and the literature of power — touching fundamental truth. It may be said, perhaps, that this famous distinction doesn't go quite to the root of the matter; De Quincey does not see clearly that the dynamic element in writing which he calls power is always emotion, and that he is really distinguishing, not between two kinds of literature, but between literature and science. Yet the passage is one of the most suggestive in modern critical writing; and you will hardly read a half-dozen pages in these literary papers without getting some such fillip to your thinking.

It must be admitted that De Quincey's literary theory is frequently warped or narrowed by his personal preferences. Every critic, I suppose, is inclined to mistake the dictates of his own taste for universal laws; De Quincey was especially liable to this error. He too often assumes that the forms of excellence he himself had attained or appreciated are the standards of all good writing. For example, he pronounces the essential and preëminent virtue of style to consist in the vital connection of successive sentences, not merely the mechanical linkings of grammar and rhetoric, but the way in which each sentence seems to beget the next, so that the thought seems growing before you as you read. To use his own pet word — which be borrowed from Coleridge — a good style is before all things "sequacious." He thinks Lamb's writing lacks this virtue; he criticises Johnson for the want of it; while he finds it the secret of Burke's undoubted mastery. Well, this is certainly a merit of good writing; and it is just the merit especially necessary and especially difficult with a habit of thought like De Quincey's. For to render the nice distinctions of his analysis, the subtle blendings of his feeling, the vague shapes of his fancy, and at the same time to follow the devious course of his reflection, to call back the digressions that dart out constantly to either side of the line of his discussion, to herd the wayward multitude of his thoughts into something like unity and keep them moving in one direction, — all this not only demands a vast vocabulary, but it strains to the utmost the mechanics of rhetorical connection. De Quincey was past-master in all the arts of excursus, parenthesis, transition, what the rhetoricians call "explicit reference." He uses more dashes to the page than any other prose-writer of equal eminence, and yet you never quite get lost in his paragraph. He was pardonably proud of having attained this particular virtue of style in such high degree; but he forgot that an author of different mental habit might have no need for it, and that most delightful English may be written which is not at all "sequacious." And what was worse, his insistence upon this virtue blinded him to the importance of some others. He blamed Johnson for always looking backward upon his thought, for framing his sentences mentally one by one before he uttered them. But we may blame De Quincey for an opposite and perhaps a worse fault; his thought does grow under his handling, but we never know whereunto it will grow. He doesn't know himself. He has no foresight of the end from the beginning. The result is that his writing is often quite formless. His essay is seldom a clear-cut, well-shaped thing. There is no outline in his work, and hence no symmetry.

The authors he himself most admired and imitated are early seventeenth-century prose men, especially Jeremy Taylor and Sir Thomas Browne. He has their volume, their elaborate stateliness of movement. Sometimes he reproduces, consciously or unconsciously, the very imagery and rhythm of some great passage in his models. Every one who has read them will remember the solemn words with which Walter Raleigh closes his *History of the World* : —

"O eloquent, just, and mighty Death! Whom none could advise, thou hast persuaded; what none hath dared, thou hast done; and whom all the world hath flattered, thou only hast cast out of the world and despised; thou hast drawn together all the far-stretched greatness, all the pride, cruelty, and ambition of man, and covered it all over with these two narrow words, 'Hic Jacet'!"

It is impossible to doubt that De Quincey had these magnificent lines in memory when he wove that famous purple patch which closes one section of the *Confessions:* —

"O just, subtle, and all-conquering opium! that to the hearts of rich and poor alike, for the wounds that will never heal, and for the pangs of grief that tempt the spirit to rebel, bringest an assuaging balm; eloquent opium! that with thy potent rhetoric stealest away the purposes of wrath, pleadest effectually for relenting pity, and through one night's heavenly sleep callest back to the guilty man the visions of his infancy and hands washed pure from blood; O just and righteous opium! that to the chancery of dreams summonest, for the triumphs of despairing innocence, false witnesses, and confoundest perjury, and dost reverse the sentences of unrighteous judges; — thou buildest upon the bosom of darkness, out of the fantastic imagery of the brain, cities and temples, beyond the art of Phidias and Praxiteles, beyond the splendors of Babylon and Hekatompylos; and 'from the anarchy of dreaming sleep,' callest into sunny light the faces of long-buried beauties, and the blessed household countenances, cleansed from the 'dishonors of the grave.' Thou only givest these gifts to man; and thou hast the keys of Paradise, O just, subtle, and mighty opium!"

This is De Quincey's best manner; every epithet justly chosen, disclosing sudden glimpses of vast, vague imagery, filled with a lofty melancholy, and moving with a slow and solemn stepping rhythm. And everybody knows that there are near a score of such passages in De Quincey's pages. If they are inferior to the best things in Taylor and Browne,— and they are, — it is only because De Quincey is just a little grandiose. It is art, not nature. He is building the lofty line; whereas the rhetoric of Taylor or Browne is natural, inevitable — they can no other. And here again De Quincey falls into the error of measuring all literature by the quality he most admires. He pronounces this lofty, ornate manner the supreme, distinctive rhetorical excellence. Rhetoric, he says, is "the art of aggrandizing and bringing out into strong relief, by means of various and striking thoughts, some aspect of truth which of itself is supported by no spontaneous feelings, and therefore rests upon artificial aids." Such a definition makes of rhetoric an artifice rather than an art, a means of giving extrinsic interest to truth rather than of disclosing its inherent power and beauty. It describes pretty accurately much of De Quincey's writing, but it does not apply with any precision even to the elaborate manner of Taylor and Browne, and still less is it a good definition of rhetoric in general. And if it is said that De Quincey is here using the term "rhetoric" in a technical sense, as denoting a special form of literary effect, it must still be urged that some such definition is assumed in his critical verdicts upon all sorts of writing. He had no feeling for the charm or the strength of simplicity. He complains of Lamb that "the gyrations within which his sentiment wheels are the briefest possible," and that he "sinks away from openings suddenly offering themselves to flights of pathos or solemnity"; forgetting that he, Thomas De Quincey, might well have afforded to pay a king's ransom if he could have written a single page of such English as Lamb's *Dream Children.* His remarks upon the style of Swift are absurd, assuming as they do that the only form of English to be admired is that of the Opium-Eater. Any honest skipper, he says, can write like Gulliver, but supposing Swift had been set to write a pendant to Raleigh's great apostrophe to Death — quoted above — "what sort of a ridiculous figure," cries he, "would your poor, bald Jonathan have cut?" Yes, and suppose, as Leslie Stephen suggests, Thomas De Quincey had been set to write another *Drapier's Letter?* If any man thinks himself able to write as Jonathan Swift wrote, he may very easily convince himself of his error by trying it. Swift meant business. He wasn't writing in an opium revery. His style is hard as nails. It was written for shop-keepers; but it frightened kings and ministers, and it will be found good stuff after most of De Quincey's purple patches have gone to the rag-bag of oblivion.

These remarks may suggest De Quincey's limitations as a critic. He has been much admired in that capacity. His editor and biographer, Mr. Masson, pronounces him *facile princeps* among the critics of his generation; but this is extravagant, even for an admirer. He certainly gives us many penetrating glimpses into the philosophy of criticism, but in the ability to apply critical principles to the interpretation or estimate of particular works, in sanity of judgment and breadth of appreciation, he is by no means the equal, I should hold, of Coleridge, Hazlitt, or Lamb. Merely as a reviewer, Jeffrey is the better man. For that kind of work De Quincey had no liking. He preferred to study the man rather than the book. In fact, he says in the opening passage of his essay on Wordsworth's poetry, 1845, that up to that time he had "never attempted an examination of any man's writings." He made no critical estimate of any of the great poets contemporary with himself. Even of the writers he admired most, the early seventeenth-century men, he has left no careful critical study. Milton, one thinks, is the English poet he might have discussed with most sympathy and illumination; but he has no criticism on Milton's work except two or three fragments of little value. In his professed critical papers, as in the biographical, he is on the hunt for something recondite, and loses no opportunity to start a train of ingenious conjecture. He overreaches himself by his own subtlety, and often fails in the first requisite of the critic, a sympathetic perception of the central quality of his author. Acute and suggestive, he is nevertheless always liable to sacrifice his grasp of a work as a whole to the discussion of some finicky detail. And occasionally his verdicts are simply perverse or freakish; the essay on Pope is full of such.

Moreover, the range of his critical appreciation was sharply limited. He was as insular as the most hide-bound Briton. The manners of all the Latin races, he says, are based on a want of principle and a want of moral sensibility. He never would admit that anything good came out of France. In speaking of the relations of French and English literature he declares that "no section whatever of French literature has ever availed to influence in the slightest degree or to modify our own"; a statement that betrays either such ignorance or such obstinate prejudice as to discredit whatever he has to say of our eighteenth-century writers. Nor is it race prejudice only that narrows his vision. As a critic of poetry, he was deficient in the sense of form, and, in spite of the pretensions of his own prose-poetry, he was deficient in the sense of rhythm. The music of verse appealed to him only when it was organ-like, Miltonic. In truth, the only two elements

in literature he ever really cared much for were the
mysterious or recondite, and the sublime; and he
liked best that writing in which the two were somehow combined. Those masterpieces of literature
which depict broad, simple action from obvious
motives had no interest for him. He lived half his
life in Edinburgh; but I find no positive evidence
that he ever read his Walter Scott. Even the sublime he did not appreciate unless there were something grandiose or spectacular in it, something
more properly to be called magnificent. Milton
he thought sublime; Homer, not at all. I doubt
whether he thought the first verse of the first chapter
of Genesis sublime; I can imagine what a rhetorical
bravura he would have written upon it. In short,
he narrowed greatly the range of his criticism by
renouncing at once half the material out of which
the best literature must be wrought — the lucid,
obvious truths of life; and then by holding per-
sistently to a conception of rhetoric which tended
to confound art with artifice.

But it is in the second of the three groups into
which all De Quincey's writing may be divided
that we shall find the work that he himself most
prized, and that is probably most interesting to
readers of to-day. Here we may place all those
passages that are the immediate product of his

imagination, — the dreams and visions of the *Confessions* and the *Suspiria de Profundis ;* the records of his childhood in which memory passes so insensibly into revery that he cannot tell what was fact and what was dream; narratives like those of the *English Mail Coach*, in which the story is enveloped in an atmosphere half feeling and half fancy; and those *Dream Echoes* in which some of the intenser moments of experience repeated themselves in image and music. This visionary gift was not due chiefly to his opium. "Habitually to dream magnificently," he says, "a man must have a constitutional determination to revery." That is what De Quincey always had. He was a dreamer by nature. His imagination loved to luxuriate in vast, dim-lighted spaces, in vague and awesome revery. He himself accounted this faculty as one of our most precious endowments, and lamented its inevitable decline under the pressure and hurry of our material age.

"Let no man think this a trifle. The machinery for dreaming planted in the human brain was not planted for nothing. That faculty, in alliance with the mystery of darkness, is the one great tube through which man communicates with the shadowy. And the dreaming organ, in connection with the heart, the eye, the ear, composes the magnificent apparatus which forces the infinite into the chambers of a human brain, and throws dark reflections from eternities below all life upon the mirrors of that mysterious *camera obscura* — the sleeping mind."

The *Confessions*, he averred, were written originally with a view to revealing the power of dreaming that is latent in every man; and this mood of lofty revery recurs frequently throughout all his later writing. The most effective passages of this sort are those most spontaneous, when the imagination in solemn forms, touched with some vague melancholy, rises directly out of some deep or intense emotion; like that hollow Memnonian sound heard at the bedside of his dead sister, or those cloudy visions of palm trees and vanishing faces in the far vault of heaven that haunted him after his sister had gone. The *Dream Echoes* and parts of the *Suspiria* are more artificial and hence less impressive. One has a suspicion that De Quincey is forcing his mood a little — at least inviting it.

It is these more studied passages that best exemplify the peculiar literary form in which, by striking imagery and especially by a certain imposing rhythm, De Quincey attempted to secure the effects of poetry without the use of metre. It is to be doubted, however, whether the attempt is altogether successful,

much as De Quincey prided himself upon it. Metre
is not an arbitrary accompaniment of poetry, a
separable ornament; it is the poet's natural voice.
The attempt, therefore, to dispense with it, while
retaining the imagery and heightened emotion of
poetry, inevitably produces a sense of artificiality.
You get a kind of bastard product, neither prose nor
verse and without the charm of either one. There
is, moreover, a special reason why such passages
as these should be in verse. It seems to be only the
musical element in speech that can lay the question-
ing intellect asleep and take us into the mood of
dream. Surprise — which is a sudden shock to
reason — is never known in dreamland. We are
terrified there, or delighted to the verge of ecstasy;
but nothing seems improbable to us until after we
have waked. It is in such a temper, if I mistake
not, that we read Shakespeare's *Midsummer-Night's
Dream* or Coleridge's *Ancient Mariner*. And the
effect in either case would be impossible without
the exquisite music of the verse which enchants us
and deludes. But De Quincey's *Dream Echoes*
hardly produce any such sense of illusion. They
lay no spell upon our reason. They are evidently
composed. De Quincey says, "Go to, I will now
dream dreams." We see how he does it; he is
making a revery.

From such strictures one passage must be excepted,

— and it is a great exception, — the vision of the "Three Ladies of Sorrow." Cut away the introductory paragraphs about Levana and the needless paragraph of personal application at the end, cut away the rubbishy footnotes, and you leave these three figures standing sad and stately in our imagination. This is not a dream begotten of opium upon idle fancy; here the imagination of De Quincey has wrought upon the deepest experiences of universal humanity. These three — Mater Lachrymarum, Mater Suspiriorum, Mater Tenebrarum — they may not yet have crossed our path, we may not yet have heard their voice; but some glimpse as from a distance, some shadow of their awful forms, every son of man has known or some day shall know. As has been truly said, they are an addition to the mythology of the human race, as solemn as the Fates or the Furies. But nowhere else has De Quincey done anything quite like this.

But after all, perhaps there is nothing in the whole body of De Quincey's work more valuable than his rambling papers of personal reminiscence; and there is pretty certainly nothing more diverting. It is to them we must look for a series of intimate portraits of some of his most important contemporaries, in their habit as they lived. The shy and retiring little man loved to study his friends in the homely circumstance of their daily life, divested of

their robes of state or of song. He had an almost
feminine nicety of observation that nothing escaped,
and a quick eye for those slight peculiarities of
appearance and manner in which character unconsciously reveals itself. Without his *Recollections* our
picture of the group of poets in the Lake District
would lose almost all its vivid details. It is gossip,
to be sure, but the gossip of a scholar and a thinker,
who sees the significance of what to others would
seem trifles. Doubtless the naïve frankness with
which he put his gossip into print was sometimes
sufficiently annoying to the subjects of it. For he
could now and then descend to mere tittle-tattle,
flavored with a little half-conscious personal malice.
Like Mr. Boswell, De Quincey would probably
have declared himself unwilling to "mitigate the
asperity of his portraits" to please anybody; yet
I suspect it was not solely to his pure love of truth
that we owe the information that Mr. Wordsworth
had bad legs and drooping shoulders; that there
was a curious variation in the brilliancy of his eyes,
due probably to the condition of his stomach; that
he was constitutionally so rigid of nature that people
wondered how he could ever have condescended to
the humiliations of courtship; that in Mrs. Wordsworth's eyes — those "stars of twilight fair" — there
was considerable obliquity of vision, which ought to
have been repulsive and yet was not; that Dorothy

Wordsworth had refused several offers of marriage, one, to his personal knowledge, from Hazlitt (which probably was not the fact) — and much other matter of this sort, perhaps beneath the dignity of full-dress biography. It is likely, however, that such details, though doubtless censured by our superior sense of propriety, add to our interest in De Quincey's story. Of course it was wrong of him; but our human curiosity often enjoys what our more rigid judgment may not approve. And what a thoroughly human, lifelike picture it is! There *was* a Wordsworth the Stamp Distributor as well as a Wordsworth the Poet; and I, for one, am glad to know both. As to Dorothy Wordsworth, the most genuinely poetic character in the group, De Quincey's account of her is worth all the rest that has been written of her. And Coleridge, to whom he was never quite so just, Southey, Wilson, Charles Lloyd, the Simpsons, and the rest, they are all real and living in his garrulous page.

One closes an essay on De Quincey with some misgivings as to its justice. But a critic may plead, in excuse for his imperfect appreciation, that there are few writers of whom a just estimate is so difficult. Few have put so much thinking into their work to so little purpose. He is certainly very full of matter. What he might have accomplished if the subtle spirit of opium that colored his dreams had

not robbed him of the power of systematic and fruit-
ful thinking, it is impossible to say.   As it was, he
had no message to deliver; he did not influence in
any wise the thought of his age; he left no work in
which vital truth takes on finished shape, or any of
the great forces of life are presented in the forms of
a healthy imagination.   I should hold, therefore,
that, while he was a most curious personality and
a very remarkable writer, he can hardly rank with
such masters of modern prose as Thomas Carlyle
and John Ruskin.

JOHN WILSON

I

DE QUINCEY, in his delightful recollections of the English lakes, relates that one night, about three hours past midnight, a young man, as yet pretty nearly a stranger to the Lake Country, — but I suppose it was the Opium-Eater himself, mooning about after this custom, — had strolled up to White Moss Common above Grasmere Lake, when he was startled by a wild bull that came puffing and laboring up the mountain road. A moment later there appeared in chase three horsemen, and the bull turned and plunged down to the marshy ground at the head of the lake, but soon dislodged thence, came forging up the hill again. The leading horseman, a towering figure crowned by a flood of yellow hair, and grasping a wooden spear fourteen feet long, now shouted, "Turn that villain, turn that villain, or he will take to Cumberland!" De Quincey turned the bull, — or says he did; I always have had my doubts about that, — and the cavalcade rushed past in the dim light of the morning, leaving him wondering whether they were not creatures of vision and dream.

This, if I am right in thinking the "young man" of the story to be De Quincey himself, was his first meeting with John Wilson. It was a very characteristic one; John Wilson was usually on some high horse, and riding at a reckless pace. Only about a year before, in 1807, twenty-two years of age and just out of the University, he had come to live at Elleray on Lake Windermere. He had made a record for brilliant though desultory scholarship in Oxford, had inherited from his father a handsome fortune, had more health and high spirits than he knew what to do with, and so now, with no very definite purpose or career in mind, he selected one of the loveliest spots in England and sat himself down to enjoy the goods of life. Few men ever had a keener relish for all the healthy pleasures of a rational animal. A goodly man to look upon. Standing full six feet, broad-chested, sinewy; shaking back from his massive forehead his dishevelled mane of tawny hair; a resonant voice and a resistless vigor in his movements, — he seemed a big, good-natured Goth. At the University he was remembered for his prowess and a certain genial impudence rather than for any more distinctively academic attainments. He had measured twenty-three feet in a running jump; after a dinner in London one night he had

167

covered the fifty-nine miles back to the college in nine hours; he had knocked out the toughest pugilist in Oxford. Here in his life at Elleray as a country gentleman, he prided himself on keeping all his manly accomplishments well in practice. "A fine, gay, girt-hearted fellow," said one of his rustic neighbors, "as strang as a lion, and as lish as a trout, an' he had sic antics as never man had."

But he was a very soft-hearted giant, whose exuberant sentiment was always running over into sentimentality. From his earliest manhood his emotions were effusive rather than steady, and his actions were largely decided by impulse. During his first college year he had formed an attachment for a certain Margaret, which seems to have been genuinely impassioned and lasted some seven years. But his mother, for some unexplained reason, was unalterably opposed to their union; and Wilson, like Gibbon, sighed as a lover and obeyed as a son. Which would seem to indicate, either that the mother had an unusually strong will, or the son an unusually weak one; it probably indicates both. Wilson certainly sighed a good deal; memory of his early passion frequently gives a sentimental tinge to his later writing — especially in the paper entitled *Streams*. But not long after taking up residence at Elleray, he met a high-spirited girl, the belle of the Lake District, of a temperament well fitted to sympathize with his own. John Wilson and Jane Penny were married in 1811, and their domestic life for twenty-five years exhibits all that is best in Wilson's character.

These early years at the lakes, however, gave little promise of public work of any sort. He had cherished since his college days some literary aspirations, and chose his residence at Elleray partly on account of the neighborhood of Wordsworth, Southey, and Coleridge. The year after his marriage he published a thin volume of dilute, sentimental verse, which most readers to-day will pronounce hardly worth while. But the life at Elleray was too full and satisfying to admit any strenuous ambitions; it was only a lucky stroke of misfortune that threw him upon his own resources and forced him to show what stuff there was in him. In 1815, through the mismanagement or treachery of a friend, he lost practically the whole of his fortune. The blow, however, was not crushing; his mother, whose fortune was not impaired, was living in her own house in Edinburgh, and invited her son with his family to take up residence with her. Wilson accepted the invitation, and the same year was called to the bar. His legal experience was neither very extended nor very remunerative; but his year and a half of "walking the Parliament House" served to bring him into acquaintance with a little group of young

Edinburgh men, one of whom was that brilliant and audacious genius soon to be associated with him in the decisive work of his life, John Gibson Lockhart.

Another of Wilson's new acquaintances was young William Blackwood, whose handsome new shop in Princess Street was just then a favorite resort of bookish people. Mr. Blackwood was a man of energy and ideas. He had succeeded in building up a prosperous business as a bookseller, and he was Edinburgh agent for the great Mr. John Murray of London; but his ventures as a publisher thus far had not been so successful. His rival, Constable, had captured the two most famous publications of the early century, the *Edinburgh Review* and the Waverley Novels. Nothing daunted, however, Blackwood risked a new venture. He determined to have a periodical of his own, Tory in politics to match the Whig *Edinburgh*. He wisely decided not to compete with the *Edinburgh* in its own field, but to make his periodical a magazine rather than a review, inviting the ablest and most brilliant contributors, but admitting a wider variety of composition and more vivacity of treatment than would be appropriate in the staider pages of a review. Unfortunately, he at first accepted as editors two men quite incompetent to realize his ideal, who, much to his vexation, termed his ambitious magazine "our

humble miscellany," and filled up its early numbers
with dull rubbish. Mr. Blackwood stood it for
six months, when he dismissed the incapables, took
the magazine into his own hands, and looked about
for some better editors. The two young fellows,
Wilson and Lockhart, had been in his shop almost
daily for a year, and he had observed their rampant
Toryism, their brilliant talk, their wide acquaintance
with books and men. He determined to secure
their services for his enterprise, and while retaining
general supervision of the magazine himself, to
intrust to them all details of its editorial conduct.

In October, 1817, appeared the first number under
the new management, the seventh of the series, but
the first real *Blackwood's Magazine*. It came upon
the decorum of Edinburgh like a thunderclap out of
a clear sky. The public, that for six months had
found in Mr. Blackwood's innocent periodical little
more exciting than the price of pigs and poultry,
was surprised to see this harmless thing changed into
the most audacious of journals, that scattered personalities right and left and had no fear of dignities.
Edinburgh society was especially scandalized by
the last article in the number. Few people nowa-
days know or care anything about this once famous
"Chaldee Manuscript"; but seldom has any fugi-
tive magazine article created such a commotion. It
was a satirical account of Blackwood's quarrel with

his first editors and of his rivalry with Constable and the *Edinburgh;* and it introduces under a thin disguise not only Blackwood and his editors, old and new, but Constable, Jeffrey, Walter Scott, and a number of other prominent persons in the little world of Edinburgh society. It is doubtless a clever skit, but its humor — which is said to have convulsed Scott with laughter — will hardly prove irresistible to the modern reader. Its allusions are purely local, and could not have been understood outside the little circle of Edinburgh. The paper is a curious proof at once of the purely provincial character of Edinburgh literary society, and of the spirit of local mischief, of a pure lark, rather than of serious literary endeavor, with which these young fellows entered upon the new enterprise of editing a magazine. The reader of to-day, moreover, will be puzzled to know why it should have ruffled the proprieties so much. Its satirical use of Scripture phrase probably displeased some good folk, and it certainly treated the big-wigs of Edinburgh with considerable levity; but there is nothing really profane in it, nor are its personalities of a sort, one thinks, to give serious offence. But in deference to public sentiment it was withdrawn, — after it had sold off the first edition of the magazine, — and is not now to be found in most sets of *Blackwood.* In fact, there were much worse things than the

"Chaldee Manuscript" in this first number of *Black-wood*. The opening paper is a review of Coleridge's *Biographia Literaria*, probably written by Wilson. It has the boisterous manner and reckless epithet always too characteristic of his critical writing. The paper misses altogether the wealth of critical principle contained in this certainly rather formless book, and is throughout only a vulgar, derisive attack upon Coleridge himself. The author of the *Ancient Mariner*, so the critic avers, has written nothing worthy of remembrance save a few wild and fanciful ballads, yet he is "so puffed up with a miserable arrogance" that he seems to consider the mighty universe itself "nothing better than a mirror in which, with a grinning and idiotic self-complacency, he may contemplate the physiognomy of Samuel Taylor Coleridge." There are twenty pages of such stuff as this, written, as the critic avers with a pious smirk, not in the cause of literature merely, but in the cause of morality and religion, lest Mr. Coleridge should be held up as a model to the coming generation. Later on in the same number is the first of that notorious series of articles on "The Cockney School of Poets," the authorship of which has never been definitely determined, but which were probably written in part by Wilson, in part by Lockhart, and in part, also, by that swashbuckling Irishman, William Maginn. The worst of them, the infamous paper on Keats, was published in August of the next year; but they are all filled with violent personalities, and as literary criticism are practically worthless.

The utmost that can be said for much of the writing in the early volumes of *Blackwood* is that it was prompted by a certain boyish hilarity rather than by any real malignity. Determined above all things that their magazine should not be dull, the two young editors laid about them recklessly, with very little regard for precision or propriety. They were always ready for a fight or a frolic, and liked best some combination of the two. Mr. Blackwood, repeatedly threatened by suits for libel, tried now and then to put some check upon his riotous team; but he was gratified to see his magazine making a stir in the world, and usually gave them free rein. For some eight years the practical conduct of the magazine was in their hands. In 1822 they began that famous series of papers in dialogue, the *Noctes Ambrosianæ*, which contains Wilson's best work. It is not certain which of the two men is to be credited with the original conception; they seem to have contributed about equally to the earlier numbers, sometimes writing together and sometimes separately. Some assistance, though probably not much, was given by James Hogg, the Ettrick Shepherd, and Maginn — who figures as O'Doherty — seems to have had some part in a few of the more hilarious papers. But from first to last the real author of the *Noctes* was Wilson. Lockhart was never a jovial or even a genial man; there was too much gall in his humor — "the scorpion that stings the faces of men," as he was well characterized in the "Chaldee Manuscript"; but Wilson's exuberant spirits, his effusive comradeship, his profuse sentimental rhetoric, all chimed exactly with the temper of the *Noctes*. After 1820, Lockhart's intimate relations with Scott — whose daughter he had married — drew him somewhat away from the magazine; and in 1825 he went to London to assume editorial control of the *Quarterly Review*, and left the conduct of *Blackwood's* entirely to Wilson. For the next ten years it was Wilson's magazine. He decided what contributors should be admitted, and he put in whatever of his own he wished. His biographer gives a list of two hundred and thirty-nine articles written by him in these ten years, aggregating about four thousand pages.

With all his editorial work Wilson had given much time, since 1820, to the duties of another position, that, one thinks, should have called for more dignity than the young fellows in Mr. Blackwood's editorial rooms were accustomed to wear. In that year he offered himself as a candidate for the professorship of moral philosophy in Edinburgh

University. The chair had been occupied by such eminent Scottish philosophers as Dugald Stewart and Thomas Brown. Wilson's rival in the candidacy was Sir William Hamilton, who had almost every qualification for the place, while Wilson, to say the truth, had almost none. He was, moreover, known to be the leading spirit in the conduct of the periodical that for nearly three years had scandalized grave Edinburgh folk by its boisterousness and its audacious personalities. But the election was a partisan affair, and Wilson won, as a Tory — with "influence." He occupied the chair until 1852, two years before his death. He was an entertaining, sometimes an eloquent, lecturer, and the charm of his personality made him popular in the class room, as everywhere else; but it cannot be said that, either by speculation or research, he ever much widened the bounds of knowledge in his department. His first interest was always in literature; and although he lectured for more than thirty years, he never cared enough for his lectures to print anything from them, save some few papers in the *Blackwood*, most of these not of sufficient importance to be included in the collected edition of his works.

The income from his professorship, together with the liberal payments from Mr. Blackwood, soon placed him beyond financial anxiety. His estate at Elleray he had never sold, and after 1823 he was able to spend his summers there regularly, with his family about him. He genuinely loved the country; only twice in the last thirty years of his life did he go up to London. It is at Elleray that one likes best to picture him, in his later as well as in his earlier years — under the great sycamore that still spreads its venerable arms over the little cottage that had been his first and best-loved home there, watching his game-cocks and rollicking with his dogs, rowing on the lake or racing up the hill behind it with a crowd of shouting children to watch the long panorama of cloud and mountain from Orrest Head ; striding with giant pace over the road to Rydal to look in upon Wordsworth or upon that best-beloved of all the Lakers, little Hartley Coleridge, at the Nab; joining with the lusty rustics in the annual Grasmere sports, and proving himself still in the wrestling "a verra hard un to lick "; keeping the gamesome spirits of youth quite down to the verge of age. He liked all sorts and conditions of active men, and used to say he thanked God he had never lost his taste for bad company. The homely folk of the Lake Country, who only knew Wordsworth as an odd party who made verses, knew John Wilson as a "gert, good feller." His memory is still green in all the Winder-mere region.

The current of this joyous life flowed unbroken till his wife died suddenly in 1837. He was never the same man after that. His connection with the magazine had not been so close since the death of the elder Blackwood, in 1835, and his contributions, though they continued till the very last year of his life, now became much less frequent. Something of the pathos of age was coming over him. Elleray he found too lonely for summer residence. His children married, and though still living near him, went out of his Edinburgh home. He was still the big, leonine man, but his temper was mellowed very much. It is true he would never quite give up his pet aversions; he could write of Keats with unrepentant vulgarity years after Keats had gone, and could jeer at Hazlitt in the old bitter fashion. Yet the widening of the circle of his personal acquaintance to include many of his old adversaries, and the certainty that the measures he had opposed were not working disaster to the state, combined with the natural effect of age and sorrows to soften the asperity of his opinions and make him more tolerant and gentle. His one immortal sentence is characteristic of those latest years: "The animosities are mortal, but the humanities live forever." His health, which he had doubtless drawn on rather heavily, hardly fulfilled the extravagant promise of his youth. In 1852 he was forced by growing weakness to resign his chair, and two years later he died, cheerful, if not buoyant, to the last.

It was shortly before his death that he met, after long absence, his old associate Lockhart, now, like himself, pathetically broken by sorrows and bereavement, and, unlike Wilson, embittered and cynical, "a weary old man," as he said, "fit now for nothing but to shut myself up and be sulky." Four months later he followed his friend. Little, withered Mr. De Quincey, who for half a century had kept his system in a pickle of laudanum, though born in the same year as Wilson, outlived him five years, dying at the riper age of seventy-four.

II

If we would estimate the literary work of Wilson, we must credit him, first of all, with having found out how to edit a magazine. For the instant success of *Blackwood's*, as well as its continued prosperity for more than twenty years, was due more largely to Wilson than to Lockhart. There is doubtless more finish in Lockhart's work; his keen and caustic satire is cruelly effective, and he was, I think, an abler critic than Wilson. But Wilson had a more intimate sympathy with his readers, a quicker sense of what would interest or amuse them at the moment; and above all he had an exuberant vitality, an immense volume of good spirits that seemed to pervade the magazine. He may almost be said to have introduced a new style into English periodical writing; he shocked the proprieties hardly more by his matter than by his manner. His style is colloquial to the last degree; it is the man himself. The personal note is dominant, to be sure, in all the essayists of the period; but the others, Hazlitt, Lamb, De Quincey, as we have seen, recognized literary standards, admired and imitated certain literary models. Wilson, on the other hand, simply let himself go. He is sentimental, or abusive, or hilarious, as the mood takes him; but he is always rhetorical, profuse, careless of decorum. Of course in such writing you will not expect nicety of judgment, chasteness or precision of phrase. Wilson writes as the traditional Irishman played the violin, "by main strength." But there is great personal force in such a manner; it is big John Wilson talking, declaiming, jesting, shouting from the page. The unpardonable sin in the columns of a magazine is dulness; and Wilson is never dull.

As to the permanent literary value of his work, that is another matter. For one thing it was usually done in too much haste to be lasting. Acting on the convenient motto, "Never do to-day what you can put off till to-morrow," he would postpone his writing to the last moment, and then, locking himself in his study, turn off sheet after sheet, with amazing rapidity, sometimes writing a whole number of the *Noctes* at a sitting. His biographer says he once wrote fifty-six double-column pages of print for *Blackwood's* in forty-eight hours. But it is art that tells in the long run; extempore writing thrown off at such a dizzy rate could not have received much artistic care. Such a rush of manner, though it may carry you away at the moment, is likely to weary after a little. We crave some repose, some temperance of feeling, delicacy of sentiment. The very qualities that gave its buoyancy to this writing at the time are peculiarly liable to evaporate in the course of a century. The effervescent humor has lost its bubble now, and tastes a little flat on the palate. A style so highly exhilarated doesn't keep well. And what is worse, this exaggerated animation suggests something factitious; we suspect it to be got up to order, like the devotional moods some pious people induce by rubbing their hands together. The man, we say, makes too much fuss over expression, and although going at full speed, doesn't seem to get on. Nor is it only his form that suffers; his opinions are often ill-considered, his critical verdicts hasty and sometimes contradictory, his rough-and-ready censure of men and measures rash and indiscriminate. His energy has too little intellectual quality; it often seems nothing but the expression of a full and healthy physical life. We shall have to admit that in all respects Wilson was a good deal of a Philistine. I should like to have heard the late Mr. Matthew Arnold express his opinion of him — and I should like to have heard him express his opinion of the late Mr. Matthew Arnold. The amenity, the fine reserve, the urbane superiority, the distrust of enthusiasms, the aversion for the raw and the hasty — all those qualities that went to the making of our great critic would have been shocked by every page that Wilson ever wrote. One can imagine, for example, Arnold's fine contempt for the horse-play of this passage in which Wilson is commenting on that amazing critical opinion of Jeffrey's — quoted on a previous page — which puts Rogers and Campbell above all their contemporaries : —

"Two living poets, however, it seems there are who, according to Mr. Jeffrey, are never to be dead ones — two who are unforgettable, and who owe their immortality, — to what, think ye? — their elegance! That *gracilis puer*, Samuel Rogers, is one of the dual number. His perfect beauties will never be brought to decay in the eyes of an enamoured world. He is so polished that time can never take the shine out of him; so classically correct are his charms that to the end of time they will be among the principal Pleasures of Memory. Jacqueline in her immortal loveliness seeming Juno, Minerva, and Venus all in one, will shed in vain 'such tears as angels weep '

over the weeds that have in truth 'no business there'
on the forgotten grave of Childe Harold! Very
like a whale! Thomas Campbell is the other pet-
poet — the last of all the flock. Ay — he, we allow,
is a star that will know no setting; but of this we
can assure the whole world, not excluding Mr.
Jeffrey, that were Mr. Campbell's soul deified, and a
star in the sky, and told by Apollo, who placed him
in the blue region, that Scott and Byron were both
buried somewhere between the Devil and the Deep
Sea, he, the author of "Lochiel's Warning," would
either leap from heaven in disdain, or insist on there
being instanter one triple constellation. What to
do with his friend Rogers, it might not be easy for
Mr. Campbell to imagine or propose at such a critical juncture; but we think it probable that he would
hint to Apollo, on the appearance of his Lordship
and the Baronet, that the Banker, with a few other
pretty poets, might be permitted to scintillate away
to all eternity as their — tail!"

Not unamusing, and very characteristic of Wilson
in its contempt for mere elegance; but it hardly
has that high seriousness Mr. Arnold used to exact
of the critic.

But the most serious discount from the permanent
value of Wilson's work is the lack of any central
purpose. The great masters of prose, Burke, Carlyle, Newman, Ruskin, Arnold, even the novelists

as Thackeray and George Eliot, have been very much in earnest over something. You can see in all their work certain dominating ethical ideas which they are bent on imparting or enforcing. Even a Philistine with a message is likely to make the world listen to him. But Wilson, so far as I can discover, had no message. For some thirty years he read lectures on ethics — I judge pretty much the same lectures — to classes in Edinburgh University; for the rest, he wrote for *Blackwood's Magazine*. He had to keep the printer's devil in copy, and he took care that what he furnished should not be dull; but it is vivacity rather than earnestness that his writing shows. As leading editor of a pronounced Tory magazine, he was bound to observe a journalist's consistency; but while we need not question the sincerity of his views, the eagerness of his political writing seems to proceed rather from partisan feeling than from any profound conviction. He loved the stir and warmth of controversy, and with his cocksure opinions and his command of imaginative epithet, controversy was certain to be both spirited and picturesque; but he cannot be called the consistent and resolute advocate of any cause. In his miscellaneous, discursive papers, like the *Noctes*, he touches a wide variety of topics without special personal interest in any, or seeming to feel a call to convince or persuade us of anything. There is

no real urgency in the man. Even in his critical
verdicts it is difficult to trace any consistent principles. As a result, his taste was never sure. In his
own writing he never quite perceived the difference
between the humorous and the hilarious, between
comedy and buffoonery, between pathos and bathos.
He records his impressions of men and books in
lively, often in very emphatic, language; but they
are capricious and sometimes conflicting. When
in his moods he is liable to damn his most favorite
idol. If there were two authors whom he intelli-
gently and consistently admired, they were William
Wordsworth and Walter Scott. Yet one day, writing for the *Noctes*, in a freakish mood,[1] not content
with calling a certain Mr. Martin "a jackass," —
which perhaps he was, — he went on to relieve his
gall yet further by remarking that Wordsworth often
wrote like an idiot, and never more so than in his
great sonnet on Milton; that he was becoming less
known every day; that he ludicrously overrated
himself; that he had thrown no light on man's
estate; that Crabbe stood immeasurably above him
as a poet of the poor; and that the *Excursion* was the
very worst poem of any sort in the English language.
And then, as if that were not enough for one fit, a
little later in the same paper — and remember this
was in 1825, when the great Sir Walter was the god

[1] *Noctes*, No. 22, September, 1825.

of the literary world's idolatry — he declares that Scott's poetry is often very bad, and that, except when his martial spirit is up, Scott is "only a tame and feeble writer." But the week after, when his paper got into print, he was in a blue, shivering terror over what he had done, and averred in a letter to Blackwood [1] that he would rather die that night than own those passages to be his. In truth, while Wilson had physical courage in abundance, of moral courage he seems to have had very little, and when a bit frightened he could roar you as gently as any sucking dove.

III

Wilson dabbled in so many varieties of composition that it is a little difficult to classify his work. The collected edition of his writings includes, besides the *Noctes*, a volume of verse, a volume of *Tales and Sketches*, two volumes of papers called *Recreations*, but best described as Out-of-Door Sketches, and four volumes of critical and miscellaneous writing in great part culled from his contributions to *Blackwood's*. The verse need not long detain us. His longest poem, *The Isle of Palms*, which was planned and in part written as early as 1805, is interesting as being, at least in conception, an early specimen of the romantic school of poetry. It was

[1] See the correspondence in Mrs. Oliphant's *William Blackwood and his Sons*, Vol. I, Chap. 6.

probably suggested by some of Southey's big ro-
mances; the metre, at all events, is clearly reminis-
cent of Southey. It is an odd mixture of wildly
improbable incident and very sweet sentiment. On
the deck of a great ship, bound we know not whither,
are a lover and a lady; when suddenly the ship is a
wreck, and all on board are lost save those two. A
kindly fortune washes them together on some shore
where it seems inconvenient to stay, and then provides
a boat to waft them to the Isle of Palms. In this
tropic paradise they live for years, wedded by fate,
the only inhabitants of the isle. A child is born to
them, and grows to young maidenhood, a sylvan
sprite, with no knowledge of the wide world's wicked-
ness. But at last a passing ship takes them off, and
brings them safely back to Liverpool and prose, when
the husband and family, we are left to infer, settle
down comfortably with his mother-in-law in Wales.
To tell us this precious tale takes some four thousand
lines; but it is hardly exaggeration to say that Wilson
never wrote a line of genuine poetry. He lacked the
gift of compression and the gift of melody, and uni-
formly diluted his passion into a gush of lukewarm
sentiment.

Nor are the *Tales* much better. They are stories
of humble life, and most of them are meant to be
very pathetic. Their subjects are not cheerful, as
may be inferred from some of the titles — *The*

Lover's Last Visit, The Headstone, The Elder's Death Bed, Consumption, and others of the same complexion. Running through them again recently, I computed that they average almost exactly two and one-half deaths to each tale — which is depressing. Besides this high mortality there is a large assortment of childless widows, broken hearts, forsaken maidens, family Bibles, churchyards, and deserted cottages. When Wilson makes an attempt upon our sensibilities he is not to be satisfied with any halfway effects. The obverse of any healthy pathos is usually humor; but Wilson seems afraid of mixing them, and there is hardly a gleam of humor in these *Tales*. It is to be feared, however, that to see this boisterous sentimentalist grow willowy and lachrymose sometimes does provoke from the irreverent reader a smile. His style, too, is not realistic or natural, but rhetorical and melodramatic. Fancy a peasant girl as she meets a friend she has not seen for some time breaking out after this fashion: —

"For mercy's sake! Sit down, Sarah, and tell me what evil has befallen you! For you are white as a ghost. Fear not to confide anything to my bosom; we herded sheep together on the lonesome braes — we have stripped the bark together in the more lonesome woods; we have played, laughed, sung, danced together; we have talked merrily and gayly, but innocently enough surely, of sweethearts together; and, Sarah, graver thoughts, too, have we shared, for when your poor brother died away like a frosted flower, I wept as if I had been his sister; nor can I ever be so happy in this world as to forget him. Tell me, my friend, why are you here, and why is your face so ghastly?"

"A plague upon sighing and grief," says Falstaff, "it blows a man up like a bladder!" Wilson's sentimental style seems to have suffered in that way. It is not full; it is inflated, dropsical. There is none of the strength of reticence in it, none of the simplicity of nature. All his sentimental writing, indeed, is lush; the Scotch have a word that often fits it still better — it is "wersh."

Among the miscellaneous writings are several papers of a purely critical character, of which the most important are those on Burns, on Coleridge, on Wordsworth (made up of several shorter notices fused into one) on Macaulay's *Lays of Ancient Rome*, and the once famous — or notorious — review of Tennyson's first volume. None of these can be given a very high place in the body of English critical literature. Wilson's opinions, as we have seen, depended greatly on his moods, and we never can be quite sure that the verdict of to-day is not to be contradicted by the verdict of to-morrow. His criticism is based on no defined principles, and of necessity, therefore, is often arbitrary and capricious. Indeed, he seldom makes any attempt at systematic and reasoned estimate of the work under examination; he simply sets down — usually in very pronounced fashion — his own impulsive feeling about his author. His criticism is the record of John Wilson's likes and dislikes. Hence it is likely to be very exaggerated and very diffuse. In the 1834 paper on Coleridge — which may have been designed as a kind of apology for the scurrilous article that opened the first number of *Blackwood's* — he occupies near a score of pages with quotations and mere rhapsodical eulogy thereon. Two-thirds of the paper on Macaulay's *Lays of Ancient Rome*, one of the best of his reviews, is taken up with rambling talk about the younger contemporary poets. Everywhere he gossips and comments, rather than interprets. But, at all events, his criticism, though sometimes wrongheaded, is sincere and hearty. It is never the dry, technical jargon of the professional critic. Wilson's appreciation was certainly limited. He liked sentiment and action in their pronounced forms; he disliked weakness, prettiness, over-refinement. It was inevitable that this big-chested critic with a voice like a megaphone, who admired Macaulay's drumand-trumpet *Lays*, should think little of John

Keats, and should deride the owls and mermen, and "airy, fairy Lillians" of young Mr. Alfred Tennyson. Yet within his limits, if we will make allowance for occasional personal prejudice, Wilson's appreciations and aversions are quite intelligible, and command our interest if not always our agreement. When he heartily enjoys a book, his comments are sure to be stimulating, and are sometimes really incisive. And even when he has a mind to scourge, so long as he is only recounting his own genuine feeling, and not feeding some personal or political spite, he seldom goes far wrong. Tennyson not unnaturally took umbrage at the roughness with which Blackwood handled his maiden volume; but it may be noticed that the ripening taste of the poet removed from the second edition of the volume most of the poems on which "crusty Christopher" had laid his big finger. In a word, Wilson is a pleasant commentator, but not a great critic. His spontaneous judgments are usually well enough; he is not always wise when he attempts to justify them. Indeed, much of his best literary criticism is to be found in the brief, incidental comment and opinion scattered through his miscellaneous writings. There are many of these excellent *obiter dicta* in the *Noctes*.

Far better than the tales or the criticism are the out-of-door papers. In them Wilson is nearly at his very best. To be sure, here as everywhere, Christopher seems in a state of over-exhilaration. His fancy is too flamboyant, and his manner vagarious to the last degree. In the course of half an hour's walk his remarks will range from the nature of Deity to the best breed of game-cocks, and leave you hardly a moment to look about you. In the midst of a hunting excursion in the wild Highland Glen Etive he cannot repress a full quarter-hour sermon — apparently to his dogs. Yet in these papers there is nothing factitious; the enthusiasm is not forced. They are full of space and breeziness. Christopher is in the open, where he was born to be, and the fresh air goes to his head. Mr. Saintsbury pronounces Wilson's descriptions of scenery better than anything of the kind in English prose; but I think he must have forgotten a good deal to say that. I should rather say that Wilson had not in any high degree the gift of description proper. There are, to be sure, many vivid and beautiful glimpses in his pages; but, as a rule, he does not set the landscape before you. What he can do is to make you feel his own joy in it. In reality he is not describing the scene, he is relating his own experience. Any one who had never taken the walk from Ambleside to Grasmere by the west bank of Rydal would hardly be able to form any picture of it from Wilson's paper, *A Stroll to Grasmere;* but to one who knows and loves that loveliest of English walks, the paper will be a delight, recall-

ing at every sentence some fair glimpse or cherished
memory. Similar comment might be made upon the
fancy-touched picture of Edinburgh in *The Moors*,
or the various scenes in the *Day on Windermere*.
And, although Wilson was an out-of-door man, he
never had the keen eye of the naturalist, or the love
for particular forms and phases of nature. He was
no Thoreau, who could "name all the birds without
a gun," and was in league with the trees of the field.
Wilson always loved nature in her larger masses and
more striking aspects. Moreover, he never cared
much for still life. His scene is usually the setting
for some form of strenuous activity. He must have
walking, and riding, and rowing, and swimming,
and hunting, and fighting, — all the joys of healthy
animal life. His love for horses and dogs makes
many pages of very good reading. I don't know
whether this generation reads any longer Christopher's account of his ride on Colonsay; but if it
doesn't, more's the pity. Old Colonsay is one of
the best horses that have ever got into books. While
as to the dog Flo, his glorious encounter with the
drunken carter's mastiff, and the general engagement
that followed between the schoolmaster with his boys
and the village tradesmen on the one side, and the
infuriated carters with a gang of gypsies and a band
of brawny Irishmen on the other — that is a classic,
one of the best fights in literature. In all these

outdoor papers Wilson's animation is contagious. You shall not read a dozen pages without an access of health, a tightening of muscle, a new realization

"How good is man's life, the mere living! How fit to employ
All the heart, and the soul, and the senses forever in joy!"

But it is in the *Noctes* that we must look for the fullest display of Wilson's powers. Here his imagination, his wisdom, his satire, his pathos, his exuberant humor, are all seen at their best. Nothing else so well shows his almost marvellous affluence and volubility. It can hardly be necessary to explain that the *Noctes* are a series of papers in dialogue, recounting the converse of a jovial company of Blackwood's men who are supposed to meet for an occasional night of good fellowship around the table of a famous Edinburgh tavern, Ambrose's — whence the name, *Noctes Ambrosianæ*. It is not certain with whom the plan of the series originated. His friends were inclined to claim that credit for William Maginn, the boisterous Irishman who figures, as Ensign O'Doherty, rather more prominently than any one else in the first eight or ten numbers. Professor Ferrier, Wilson's editor, on the other hand, is confident that the suggestion came from Wilson, though he will not admit the first eighteen papers to the collected edition of the *Works*. Whoever planned the *Noctes*, the first half-dozen numbers give scanty evidence of Wilson's genius. After that there are, I think, increasing marks of his hand, and when, about 1825, he took the series entirely under his control, the papers gain immensely both in manner and content. After about that time most of them were written entirely by him, and his temper dominates them all. He also changed the plan of the series so as to give it greater unity, and some individuality to the speakers. The early papers introduced a considerable number of persons, of various sorts and conditions, and the speech and manner of each were imitated with only very moderate success. Wilson wisely abandoned this attempt to represent with dramatic fidelity many different persons, and reduced the speakers to three: Christopher North, who stands for Wilson himself; Tickler, who is said to have been suggested by an uncle of Wilson, Robert Sym; and the Ettrick Shepherd, James Hogg. There is, indeed, no very distinct individuality in these three; they are only three persons in one John Wilson. But they enabled Wilson to express different sides of his character, different phases of his feeling. Christopher North, who speaks chiefly as a kind of interlocutor to suggest or guide the talk, is Wilson in his staider moods, with a tendency to philosophic reflection in rhetorical forms; Tickler is Wilson in his occasional moods of prosaic common sense, trying to be a man of affairs with a vein of cynicism; the Shepherd is Wilson the poet and humorist letting himself go. Naturally, therefore, the Shepherd is the most interesting of the trio, and comes nearest to being an independent character. He was doubtless studied directly, though very freely, from the original. Hogg had been an occasional contributor to *Blackwood's* ever since the famous "Chaldee Manuscript," — of which he claimed to be the author, — and by 1825 was one of the most picturesque figures in Edinburgh literary society. The real Hogg, however, was clearly very much idealized in the Shepherd of the *Noctes*, and in some of his letters shows an odd mixture of vanity and vexation at seeing himself translated into so large a type.

The colloquy as a literary form has some manifest advantages. It enables you to prove anything, by making one of the disputants a man of straw. It is also an excellent device for self-flattery. You have only to divide yourself into two persons and then let each flatter the other. North is forever admiring the Shepherd's rhapsodies or dissolving in tears at his pathos; while the Shepherd is forever holding up his hands in awe at North's eloquence. "O man, man! but ye're an orator — the orator o' the human race!" Certainly a manner so discursive and rambling as Wilson's found in the *Noctes* the best possible form of expression. Impulsive, sentimental, he had little power of connected thinking, and could rarely keep himself to one theme for ten minutes together.   But in the jovial evenings around the board at Ambrose's, connected thinking would be only another name for dulness.   Politics, criticism, philosophy, sentiment, fancy, are mixed in this rushing flow of talk and enlivened by jest, and story, and song.   Within a half-dozen pages you may come upon a résumé of German contemporary philosophy, an account of a dog fight, an estimate of Wordsworth's poetry, a scathing denunciation of the Cockney school of poetry, a bravura of sentimental rhetoric over a Scotch moonrise, and a comic song; and the whole fairly boiling and bubbling with good spirits.   Possibly the modern reader may suggest that something of the exhilaration of the *Noctes* is due to spirits of another brew.   Wilson, like old Ben Jonson, was no man to sing

> "My mind to me a kingdom is,
>   While the lank hungry belly cries for food,"

and the amount swallowed, both of solids and liquids, at each of the *Noctes* is certainly something enormous.   I believe Mr. Saintsbury (who rather prides himself as an authority upon such matters) pronounces the Gargantuan exploits at Ambrose's table quite within the limits of possibility, only suggesting that there were too many oysters for the Glenlivet.   On these questions I pretend to no opinion; but I well remember the shock of mild surprise my callow youth received on first reading the *Noctes*, on the recommendation of a worthy doctor of divinity much enamoured of them. And I still incline to doubt whether the less valorous appetites of to-day will quite assent to the confident assertion of the Shepherd: "There does not at this blessed moment breathe on the earth's surface ae human body that doesna prefer eating and drinking to all ither pleasures o' body or soul. . . . Eat an drink wi' all your powers — moral, intellectual, and spiritual. This is the rule." The Shepherd follows his rule very closely. On a fair computation, about a quarter of all the talk in the *Noctes* is devoted to meats and drinks and the effects thereof.

Of course all this is a Barmecide feast — only a device to afford expression for Wilson's extravagant high spirits. Ambrose's was, in fact, not at all the abode of oriental splendor it appears in Wilson's pages, but only a plain Edinburgh tavern; and if Wilson and Sym and Hogg ever did foregather there, their potations were doubtless very moderate. Their talk in the *Noctes* is by no means the talk of half-befuddled men, whose god is their belly and who mind earthly things. It is mostly very good talk indeed, playing over all sorts of subjects with quick intelligence, and glowing with fun and fancy. There are bits of excellent criticism in it, not quite dissolved in a wide welter of words. In fact, as already remarked, Wilson's literary criticism is often at its best in these incidental comments struck out in the heat of conversation. There is hardly a paper in which the Shepherd does not inquire after "onything gude in literature." The verdicts are usually very positive; books, new or old, are praised and damned without any nice qualifications of sentence. Moreover, the plan of the *Noctes* serves to disguise Wilson's frequent inconsistencies; for on such jovial occasions the opinions of the critics will naturally vary with their moods, and Wilson as Christopher must inevitably often disagree with Wilson as the Shepherd. But, taken together, the papers afford an interesting conspectus of literary news and criticism for some ten years. And there is a deal of sound sense — of a rather high Tory sort — on a great variety of other matters, on current politics and statesmen, on social questions, on education, on religion, on public morals — on all topics in which a well-fed Scot might be expected to take interest. But, of course, the suppers at Ambrose's were not intended primarily as Aids to Reflection. The great charm of the *Noctes* is the buoyant, ebullient life that pulses all through them. These men have the gift, not very common in colloquial writing, of "making you of their company anon," as Chaucer says. And if they are a little boisterous in tone, and their humor, now and then — as the Shepherd owns — "a bit coorse," yet it is the clean mirth of robust and healthy men. In these days when so much hectic, morbid, neurotic literature is offered for our recreation, it is pleasant to join sometimes the company of these red-blooded persons who don't enjoy poor health.

The Shepherd, in particular, is delightful. In his talk you get Wilson's humor, sentiment, and imagination in their superlative forms. The humor cannot be called quiet or delicate; yet the Shepherd has store of neat quips and jests, and now and then strikes out a vivid portrait in few words — as of Lockhart, "a pale face an' a black touzy head, but an ee like an eagle's, an' a sort o' lauch about the screwed-up mouth o' him that fules ca'd no canny, for they could na thole the meanin' o' 't." Some of his satiric hits are very good, as when he *hopes* there's many an incident in the *Excursion* he has forgotten, "for I canna say I reclet ony incident at all in the haill poem, but the Pedlar's refusin' to tak a tumbler o' gin an' water wi' the solitary. *That* did mak a deep impression on my memory, for I thocht it a most rude an' heartless thing to decline drinkin' wi' a gentleman in his ain house; but I hope it wasna true, an' that the whole is a meleegnant invention o'

Mr. Wordsworth." The Shepherd's anger, too, sometimes inspires passages of hearty Scottish malediction that are animating reading. But best of all are his passages of flamboyant, full-length description or narrative. The Shepherd's imagination, like his humor, is very profuse; it revels in details and lavishes adjectives. Yet the resulting picture is always real and glowing. His account of the Explosion of a Haggis, of his Robbing of an Eagle's Nest, of Christopher's Fishing, of the Glasgow Dog Fight, his contrasted description of the squalor of Morning in Old Edinburgh, and Daybreak in the Ettrick Valley, his delightful defence of Sleeping in Church, — these, with half a hundred other passages, will occur to all lovers of the *Noctes* as striking examples of the union of effusive sentiment or humor with vivid and realistic detail. They are better than the similar rhetorical fantasies and elaborate pathetic passages in Wilson's other works, because they seem more spontaneous. And, although his characteristic manner fairly runs riot in them, the Scottish dialect gives them a homely naturalness and keeps their sentiment from getting mawkish.

On the whole, we may admit that Wilson could not add much to the world's knowledge, and that he did little to champion any reform or advance. His prejudices were obstinate, his judgments often capricious or perverse. He lacked fixed and reasoned convictions; he lacked steadfast earnestness of resolve. We distrust the sanity of his opinions and the consistency of his conduct. Moreover, his mind would not work steadily at low pressure. As a result, his writing has no repose, no quiet certainty of manner; he is liable to fatigue us, after a little, by the very noise of his enthusiasm. Yet it is assuredly one of the offices of good literature to cheer and invigorate, even to amuse, as well as to inform or inspire. And few writers of his generation contributed more to the literature of cheer than Wilson. It was no slight service to keep before the public for a score of years a personality so healthy, a temperament so optimistic and joyous. His humor, to be sure, is not of the gentle variety that enlivens five o'clock tea, but it is never merely bacchanalian — which makes the dreariest of all writing. Even in the most exhilarated passages of what Carlyle unjustly calls "his drunken *Noctes*," there is far more of cheer than of inebriation. If Wilson, on the Moors or at the table of Ambrose, does not forget that man is an animal, he always remembers that he is a rational and spiritual animal. He has a healthy appreciation not only of the joys of sense, but of all the beauty of the world, and of all the manifold humors of man and womankind. It is impossible to rise from an hour with him without feeling that life is worth living, that

JOHN WILSON

"A merry heart goes all the day,
  Your sad tires in a mile-a."

In the merciless winnowing of time all of his verse, all the *Tales*, and most of the criticism will doubtless fall into oblivion — nay, have already descended thither. But the wholesome Out-of-Door Papers and the *Noctes* ought to live at least another century as part of the literature of invigoration. In them Christopher and the Shepherd are too much alive soon to die out of the memory of men who love good fellowship and hearty cheer.

LEIGH HUNT

I

LEIGH HUNT was certainly not a great writer nor a great man. One short poem, familiar to everybody, — the *Abou ben Adhem,* — and two or three other short poems that deserve to be familiar are all the verse he ever wrote of any real merit; while as to the prose, though much of it is entertaining and some of it of real value as criticism, there is no passage in the whole body of it that, either for weight of thought or finish of style, can be called classic. Much of his writing, perhaps most of it, belongs rather to journalism than to literature, entertaining to-day, forgotten to-morrow. No uniform edition of his works has ever been issued; many of the books have already fallen so far into obscurity that it is difficult to get a complete set of them together.   If his reputation is to be measured by the permanent value of the writing he has left us, he can hardly be sure of a place in our literary history.   That, doubtless, is the only ultimate measure of fame for any author; but meantime Leigh Hunt deserves to be remembered another century, not only as a pleasing writer, but as a man of original though limited genius, and of a personality that, in spite of its blemishes, certainly had a peculiar attraction for many greater men than himself. With a most hearty love for books and all bookish things, he always sought the companionship of men of letters, and his genuine kindliness, his sprightly converse, his taste, keen and delicate, if not broad or sound, always made him welcome. The cheery, chirruping, effervescent little optimist was the friend of two generations of literary men, and seems omnipresent in literary society for fifty years. Coleridge, Wordsworth, Byron, Shelley, Keats, Moore, Lamb, Hazlitt, Crabb Robinson, Haydon, Talfourd, Charles and Mary Cowden Clarke, Wilson, Lockhart, Murray, Macaulay, Forster, Dickens, Thackeray, Browning, Mrs. Browning, Lord Houghton, the Carlyles, Rossetti, William Bell Scott, Lowell, Hawthorne, Motley, — Leigh Hunt knew every one of them, and turns up somewhere in the memoirs or correspondence of every one. His own letters are perhaps quite as interesting as his other prose writing, yet it is evident that they miss the vivacity of his presence and converse. A reputation like this, based not so much upon the value of a writer's work as upon the breadth of his acquaintance and the elusive charm of his personality, is likely to leave the literary critic somewhat at a loss, or to beguile him into gossip and reminiscence.

The account of his parentage which Hunt gives in his *Autobiography* makes it evident that he came honestly by his characteristic traits both of temper and of belief. His father, Isaac Hunt, was a West Indian sent from the Barbados in his boyhood to be educated in Philadelphia. He took the degree of Master of Arts both in Philadelphia and in New York, — so his son says, — and then decided not to return to the Barbados, but to remain in America and enter the profession of law. His commencement oration in Philadelphia must have been of an eloquence rather unusual in that variety of address; for two young ladies fell in love with him on hearing it — which may have had something to do with his decision to remain in America. At all events, he married the younger of the two. The other one, by the way, married the artist, Benjamin West, and showed very substantial friendship for the Hunts in their later seasons of adversity. When the Revolutionary War broke out, Isaac Hunt's loud-spoken British loyalty exposed him to rough handling in Philadelphia, and he escaped to London, leaving his wife and child to follow some months later. Once there, he speedily exchanged law for divinity, and on her arrival in London Mrs. Hunt found her husband an eloquent preacher, with crowds of

carriages at his church door and throngs of delighted
ladies hanging on his utterances. But it was soon
noticed that the eloquent preacher drank too much
claret, and owed too much money. In truth, he had
no depth or steadiness of character. He could never
understand the nature of a financial obligation, —
a weakness that he bequeathed unimpaired to his
son, — and after the first flush of prosperity, was
always running behind the constable. Leigh Hunt
says the first room he himself remembers being
inside of was a debtor's jail. But nothing could
depress Isaac Hunt's easy good nature; he was always vivacious and hopeful, even unconcerned. As
to his religious beliefs, if he had any, they must have
been of a very gelatinous sort; he seems to have slid
easily down the scale of heterodoxy from one ism to
another, till he landed in a sort of benevolent indiffer-
entism. His son, who always showed an amiable
charity for his father's failings, says with delightful
naïveté, "While he was not a hypocrite, my father
was not, I must confess, remarkable for being explicit about himself."

But Hunt's picture of his mother, in the early
chapters of the *Autobiography*, is one of the most
beautiful tributes of filial affection in our literature;
it is impossible not to have a kindly feeling for the
man who could write it. She was a gentle, sad-
faced woman, with a liking for a little music and all

the gracious domesticities of life, and with a temperament as pensive as her husband's was mercurial.
She could not sympathize with his cheerful incapacity;
and the long struggle with poverty early wore out her
strength and her spirits. Hunt could not remember
to have seen her smile, "save in sorrowful tenderness." But she was full of pity for the hardships of
others; it was the taking off her flannel petticoat to
clothe a freezing woman she met on the street that
fixed upon her a rheumatic affection for life. As her
son truly says, "Saints have been made for charities
no greater." She imparted to her children — at all
events to Leigh — something of her own extreme
sympathy for all pain, and her own dislike of anything violent or overstrenuous, even in language.
Hunt says that when his childish anger once found
relief in a word that probably did not give the record-
ing angel much concern, he himself was tormented
by conscience for a week, and couldn't receive a bit
of praise or a pat of encouragement without thinking
to himself, "Ah, they little suspect I am the boy who
said, 'Damn it!'"

The young Leigh Hunt got his temperament
mostly from his father, and his training from his
mother. The results were not altogether fortunate.
At the age of eight he was entered at Christ's Hospital
School — just after Coleridge and Lamb had left it.
Old Dr. Bowyer — whom Coleridge declared to be

ready to flog anybody except a cherub, all head and
wings, whom he couldn't flog — was still master
there, and it might have been supposed that his
vigorous discipline, with the rough experiences of an
English boys' school, would have knocked a little
robustness into Hunt; but, on the contrary, it developed a sort of priggish gentleness not altogether
becoming a genuine boy. A square, good-natured
fight now and then would probably have been good
for him; but he refused to strike. He plumed himself on saying what he chose in any quarrel, and then
quietly taking the consequences. That was what
he called a moral victory. He said with evident
satisfaction, fifty years afterward, "I gained the
reputation of a romantic enthusiast whose daring in
behalf of a friend or a good cause nothing could
put down." It is clear enough that, even in his
school days, he began to show that jaunty humility
and pride of martyrdom which his critics later found
so exasperating. To provoke your enemy to smite
you on the one cheek in order that you may have the
proud satisfaction of meekly turning to him the other,
is not exactly the conduct enjoined by Scripture;
but Hunt dearly loved to do it, and began the practice
very early.

On leaving school at sixteen Hunt did not go on
to the University, but drifted for a time. The only
ambition he had thus far developed was to put his

name in the roll of English poets. He confesses
that he had not yet learned the multiplication
table, — indeed, I don't think he ever did quite
master that mystery, — but he had written a good
many verses; about a year and a half after leaving
school he published a thin volume of them. His
father got him a handsome list of subscribers, and
the verses were thought by some less partial critics
to be rather clever. The generous public, I believe,
bought rather more copies of them than of a volume
of *Lyrical Ballads* issued about a year before. The
success of his venture confirmed his poetical inclina-
tions, and he contributed occasional verse to various
periodicals during the next half-dozen years. But
his literary aspirations was soon turned in another
and more fortunate direction. His father gave him
— he does not say just when — a set of the eighteenth-
century essayists, of whom he had hitherto been
almost entirely ignorant. He devoured them all.
Goldsmith's papers in the *Bee* and *Citizen of the
World*, and the rather mild humor of Colman and
Thornton in the *Connoisseur*, gave him, he says, all
the transports of a first love. He set himself to
imitate these models in a series of papers for a London journal; he began to write theatrical notices; he
lost no opportunity to get himself naturalized in
Bohemia by cultivating the acquaintance of journalists, critics, and men about town; he diligently ex-

tended his reading in that kind of prose in which he was ambitious to excel. He was especially attracted by the brilliant satire and caustic wit of Voltaire; and as he could not read him in the original, went through the greater part of his writings in translation. He was not frightened, he remarks incidentally, by Voltaire's attacks on orthodoxy; as, indeed, it was impossible he should be. For before he was out of his teens, Hunt had reduced his theological creed to the one proposition that every created being is destined to eternal happiness — or, as he sometimes puts it, everything that happens must, in the long run, be best for everybody; and he rejected without much consideration any doctrines that conflicted, or even seemed to conflict, with this comfortable belief. His political creed was hardly more definite or more well considered. He only knew he was in favor of change and reform everywhere, and opposed to all institutions intrenched in privilege. This was the training and equipment he brought to his first important enterprise, the editing of a radical journal.

It was in 1808 that, in concert with his elder brother John, who was a printer, he set up a weekly paper, of which the two brothers were to be joint editors and proprietors. It will be remembered that this was the time when Austerlitz, Jena, and Friedland had carried Napoleon almost to the summit of his resistless career; when those sanguine young Englishmen who, some twenty years before, had hailed with joyful anticipation the revolutionary movement in France, had now long since given up those early hopes and gone over to the majority; when conservatism in England was having everything its own way, and to utter liberal opinions was to incur the suspicion of disloyalty to the British constitution and even risk of personal arrest. To set up a liberal paper at such a moment implied a little courage; but it also involved just that defiance of authority and chance of persecution always attractive to Hunt. The *Examiner* was not to be a dangerously radical sheet. It upheld the British constitution. It regarded the later stages of the French Revolution with abhorrence. It did not — as Hazlitt did — admire Napoleon; it rather advised England to let him alone and mind her own business — advice that England has never been very ready to take, and that was especially impracticable just then. The *Examiner* was to stand for independence and political reform at home, just when the frightened conservatism of England would hear nothing of reform. Its purposes were wise enough, but the temper in which it advocated them was sometimes a little sentimental, and usually not a little lofty. The magisterial assurance with which these young fellows — Hunt was twenty-four — rebuked and instructed statesmen and philosophers was certainly very superior. Hunt himself said, many years afterward, that he blushed at remembering the contrast between the simpleton he was and the sage he tried to seem. Yet assurance is a requisite of the editor, young or old; he must assume that virtue if he have it not. And Hunt's political writing in the *Examiner* will not, for the most part, strike the reader of to-day as especially dogmatic or impracticable.

To Hunt, however, the politics of the *Examiner* was probably of less interest than its literature. He confesses that in those days he cared more for writing verses than he cared for the public good, and would have been glad to devote himself entirely to poetry and philosophy. As it was, he determined to produce in the *Examiner*, to use his own phrase, "a fusion of literary taste with all subjects whatever." But the fusion of literary taste with radical politics in the columns of a weekly newspaper is not always easy. In 1811, after three years of success with the *Examiner*, he set up beside it a quarterly journal called the *Reflector*, which might serve as a repository for longer and more distinctively literary articles and for poetry. The *Reflector* shone only for four numbers, and is not very brilliant. By far the best things in it are three essays by Lamb, *On the Genius of Hogarth, On Shakespeare's Tragedies, On the Behavior of Married People*, and his delightful *Farewell to Tobacco*. But among Hunt's own contributions are three or four of those chatty, sentimental papers on bookish subjects which form so large a part of his best work in later years. One of them, *A Day by the Fire*, is in his very best vein.

It was in the *Reflector*, also, that Hunt printed his most ambitious attempt at poetry so far, a light satire entitled *The Feast of the Poets*. Like all his other early poetry, it is an echo; indeed, as the title implies, it is almost a parody of Sir John Suckling's *Session of the Poets*. With a young man's audacity he deals his censure right and left, and doubtless, as he said, made almost every living poet and poetaster his enemy. Only four contemporaries are found worthy to sit at the feast of Apollo — Scott, Campbell, Southey, and Moore; and the god lectures each of these in turn very roundly for the deficiencies of his work. He is especially severe upon Scott, just then, it will be remembered, at the height of his poetic fame, with all the world reading *Marmion* and the *Lady of the Lake*. As for Coleridge and Wordsworth, Apollo contemptuously shows them the door, laughing

> "between anger and mirth,
> And cried, 'Were there ever such asses on earth?'"

and when "Billy" and "Sam" are slow to go, the god puts on all his splendors and fairly dazzles them out of his presence. But the verses, though amusing, are not so clever as Suckling's; their familiarity passes into vulgarity, and their critical verdicts show no real insight. Hunt afterward admitted that when he wrote them he had not read Wordsworth at all, and knew next to nothing of Coleridge. His attack on Scott was prompted by a dislike of a single word in one of Scott's notes on Dryden. Many years later he reworked the poem, taking out the offending passages; but the new version, though quite innocuous, is quite flat. It is curious to note that Hunt's poem furnished the suggestion for the plan of a much cleverer satire, Lowell's *Fable for Critics*.

Meantime, fortune had been kind to Mr. Hunt. In 1809, emboldened by the success of the *Examiner*, he ventured to marry and set up a modest home. For with all his shiftlessness he was not a Bohemian by nature, but liked a certain domestic snugness. His marriage at twenty-five terminated an engagement contracted when he was seventeen and the lady was thirteen years of age; and through all those eight years it would seem clear from his letters that, in spite of other passing fancies, he had been a devoted lover. Mrs. Hunt seems to have been a nice young person — not pretty, her son rather ungallantly says, but with pretty tastes, for sketching, and water-colors, and embroidery, and a little poetry, and with a gift to read verses aloud quite remarkably well. It is evident from their letters that Hunt was anxious about her culture and during their engagement gave her a good deal of superior advice. One would think that during the fifty years of their married life she might have had opportunity to repay that obligation. Certainly we need not withhold our sympathy from the woman who, in constant illness and with a large family of children, maintained for half a century something like order and cheer in the household of a man of such varied ineptitude as Leigh Hunt. The two or three sayings recorded of her show that she must have had some imagination and some spirit — she said when first she saw a grove of olive trees in Italy that they "looked as if they only grew by moonlight," which is very pretty and very true; and when Byron said in her presence one day that Trelawney had been speaking against his morals, she quietly remarked, "It is the first time I ever heard of them." [1]

But it was in February, 1813, that the first great

[1] A letter written in 1899, by Hunt's physician, Dr. George Bird, and recently published (*The Nation* (London) Vol. V, No. 8, page 724, Saturday, May 22, 1909). charges Mrs. Hunt not only with feebleness and fretfulness, but with mendacity and intemperance, and ascribes to her influence most of Hunt's financial and other troubles. But I find it impossible to believe these charges in the face of Hunt's own statements in loving praise of his wife. His remarkable frankness never could conceal the weaknesses even of his nearest friends.

piece of good luck befell Hunt; he was sent to jail. The *Examiner* had from the start earned the reputation of being a very outspoken journal. It had been prosecuted three times in two years, but had thus far escaped conviction, when in 1812 appeared the famous article on the Prince Regent. Hunt had criticised this "first gentleman of England" very freely in an article of the *Reflector;* but the paper in the *Examiner* was much more caustic. Apropos of some fulsome eulogies of the Prince in the *Chronicle* and *Post*, the *Examiner* broke loose after this fashion: —

"What person unacquainted with the true state of the case would imagine, in reading these astounding eulogies, that this 'glory of the people' was the subject of millions of shrugs and reproaches; that this 'protector of the arts' had named a wretched foreigner his historical painter in disparagement or in ignorance of the merits of his own countrymen; that this 'Mæcenas of the age' patronized not a single deserving writer; that this 'breather of eloquence' could not say a dozen decent words, if we are to judge at least from what he said to his regiment on its embarkation for Portugal; that this 'conqueror of hearts' was the disappointer of hopes; that this 'exciter of desire' (Bravo, messieurs of the *Post!*), this Adonis in loveliness was a corpulent man of fifty, — in short, this delightful, blissful, wise, pleasurable, honorable, virtuous, true, and immortal prince was a violater of his word, a libertine over head and ears in disgrace, a despiser of domestic ties, the companion of gamblers, and demireps, a man who has just closed half a century without one single claim on the gratitude of his country or the respect of posterity."

All which, though he most potently and powerfully believed, Hunt should have seen it not honesty thus to have set down. Certainly no government, then or now, that would save a shred of the divinity that doth hedge a king could let such language go unpunished. After some months of the law's delay Hunt and his brother John were both sentenced to two years' imprisonment, John in Clerkenwell, and Leigh in Horsemonger Lane.

But the two years that followed were far from being the most unpleasant years of Hunt's life. He used to like to think that his imprisonment had impaired his health; but as he never had any very serious illness and lived to the ripe age of seventy-five, I think he was mistaken about that. After a few days he was given a pleasant suite of two rooms, one of which he proceeded to decorate with a wall-paper showing a lattice of roses climbing up the sides of the room, and blue sky and clouds on the ceiling, so that — like a good deal of his other work

— it must have been all very pretty and in very
bad taste. He brought into this room a choice
library — largely made up of the Parnaso Italiano —
with busts, and pictures, and his piano. His wife
was with him, so that neither his literary nor his domestic life suffered any serious interruption. In
fact, his eldest daughter and his longest poem were
both born inside the jail. He had a garden, too,
that furnished him with flowers of his own raising,
and gave him about as much exercise and as much
scenery as he ever really cared for. His friends
were allowed to write him freely. He enjoyed
enforced regularity of habit; he was boarded and
lodged — perhaps for the only time in his life —
without any anxiety from creditors; and with reading and writing and music and little dinners sent in
by friends over the way, he made it a life of elegant
retirement. On the whole, one thinks it was not a
heavy price to pay for the privilege of writing a very
telling libel and wearing a faint halo of martyrdom
in the cause of civil liberty ever after. And of
course it widened his reputation instantly. A good
many people of influence, hitherto strangers to him,
took occasion to manifest in various ways their sympathy with the persecuted champion of free speech.
Not only old friends like the Lambs and Cowden
Clarke came to visit him in prison, but Hazlitt came,
and Bentham, and James Mill, and Haydon, and

Shelley, and Byron, and Moore, and hosts of lesser folk. And when he came out, young Keats, who had not yet met him, wrote a sonnet to commemorate the event.

After his liberation Hunt felt that he might with some assurance of recognition turn his attention more exclusively to literature. Though he continued to edit the *Examiner* with his brother until 1821, he did not venture any further dangerous meddling with politics, but made his paper more largely a journal of criticism and letters. He had published in 1816 his most ambitious poem, *The Story of Rimini*, and three years later issued a collected edition of all his verse. He changed his residence — probably for reasons easily guessed — a half-dozen times in a half-dozen years; but where-ever he was, his modest home was always open to his friends, and there were flowers and music and books and endless literary chat. All lovers of Keats will remember his pleasant sonnet

> "Brimful of the friendliness
> That in a little cottage I have found" —

that little cottage in the Vale of Health where he wrote that other and better sonnet *The Grasshopper and the Cricket* and the characteristic lines *Sleep and Poetry*. Shelley, then living at Great Marlow, was through those years Hunt's close friend, and often came over to Hampstead to stay for days together. Byron condescended to call several times upon him. And Hunt's correspondence from 1816 to 1820 gives glimpses of many other pleasant people of more or less note in the world of literature, some of them old friends and some of them new, that often looked in upon him. In those days he was at his best as a companion —sprightly, vivacious, quick-witted, with a certain courtly grace of manner. He was an excellent reader and mimic, told a story capitally, sang a simple song neatly, was ready with some pert remark or pretty fancy, and had a head full of superficial ideas that he had never taken much pains to assert. Charles Cowden Clarke, who knew a great many charming people in his day, declared that Hunt was "fascinating, animated, and winning, to a degree of which I have never seen the parallel"; and the more impartial Hazlitt gives a picture of him in those days which seems as truthful as it is vivid:

"Hunt has a fine vinous spirit and tropical blood in his veins; but he is better at his own table. He has a great flow of pleasantry and delightful animal spirits, but his hits do not tell like Lamb's; you cannot repeat them the next day. He requires not only to be appreciated, but to have a select circle of admirers and devotees, to feel himself quite at home. . . . He manages an argument adroitly, is genteel and gallant, and has a set of by-phrases and quaint allusions always at hand to produce a laugh. If he has a fault, it is that he does not listen so well as he speaks, is impatient of interruption, and is fond of being looked up to without considering by whom. I believe, however, he has pretty well seen the folly of this."

This fault, however, in spite of Hazlitt's generous judgment, I think Hunt had not then outgrown — nor ever did outgrow. He was ambitious of the fame of a literary patron. He defended in the *Examiner* the character and the writings of Shelley. He commended without reservation the early volumes of Keats, that everybody else neglected or derided. But, though his praise was very genuine, it was a positive injury to both Shelley and Keats; for it was given in such a tone of patronizing personal friendship as to make it possible for the hostile critics to represent these two great poets as merely the disciples and imitators of Mr. Leigh Hunt. The abusive articles on *The Cockney School of Poets* that defiled the pages of *Blackwood's* were provoked chiefly by Hunt, and their bitterest denunciations levelled at him. Yet I think that Hunt, while justly angered by them, took a secret satisfaction at being recognized as the head and sponsor of a new school of poets. It pleased him to believe that he was now suffering as the leader of a new and liberal movement in poetry as well as in politics.

The cool reception given to his own verses even by the partial judgment of his friends ought to have shaken his conviction that he was himself a poet. Perhaps it did. At all events, after 1819, he abandoned poetry for a number of years, and, indeed, never after attempted anything ambitious in verse. Late in that year 1819, however, he tried his hand at something he had found he could do much better. He set up a paper made up mostly of essays written by himself with occasional contributions from others, and now and then some choice passages selected from an old or little known author. The *Indicator*, as he called this periodical, was issued weekly, and ran for sixty-six numbers. It contains the best specimens of that familiar, chatty essay which Hunt had begun to write in the *Reflector*, and which he wrote better than any one else. He always looked back upon it with peculiar fondness, and loved to remember that such a paper had pleased Lamb, and another Shelley, and yet another Hazlitt.

Through all these years, as always, Hunt was sadly in need of money. At some time not long after his liberation from prison Shelley had given him outright fourteen hundred pounds to extricate him from his debts; but, as he naïvely says, "I was not extricated, for I had not yet learned to be careful."

Harassed by these difficulties, increased now by the needs of a growing family and the ill-health of his wife, and finding the strain upon his own energies caused by writing nearly the whole of the *Examiner* and the *Indicator* was getting unendurable, he gave up both papers in 1821, and entered upon a new and very ill-starred enterprise. He accepted the invitation of Shelley, then in Italy, to join him and Byron there in the conduct of a new review, called the *Liberal*, to be edited in Italy but printed by John Hunt in London. It is easy to see that the scheme must have been attractive to Hunt. He accounted Shelley his best friend — with good reason. He had longed for years to see Italy. And as for the proposed review, he thought the name of Byron, then at the height of his fame, would assure its success. But the plan was unlucky from the start. A week after his arrival, Shelley met his tragic death, and Hunt, practically penniless, was thrown upon the rather cool generosity of Byron. Byron was then living at Pisa with La Guiccioli and his very nondescript menage; and for a time the Hunts attempted to lodge under the same roof. But Byron found Hunt limp and helpless, Mrs. Hunt and the children vulgar; while Hunt found Byron exacting and penurious, and Mrs. Hunt would have nothing to do with his odious establishment. Obviously the relations were impossible. The *Liberal* was started;

but Byron, never having cared much for it, now cared nothing, and would contribute nothing save matter that Murray didn't dare to publish, and John Hunt got into prison again for publishing. The first three numbers contained Shelley's fine translation of Goethe's *Walpurgis Nacht* and some other beautiful fragments he had left, and Hazlitt's inimitable paper *My First Acquaintance with Poets;* but Hunt was left without further assistance, and with the fourth number the *Liberal* died. Not long after Byron started on his Greek expedition, and Hunt was left to shift for himself. He had not money enough to take his large family back to England, and stayed on two years more in Florence, supported — Heaven knows how! Probably by his contributions to London papers, with generous contributions from Mrs. Shelley. Finally, in 1825, a London publisher advanced money enough to bring him back, and the homesick wanderer found himself again in the fields of his beloved Hampstead.

This chapter of his life would, however, not have been so very unfortunate if it had ended there. But two years later, finding it necessary to furnish something to the publisher, Colburn, in return for the money advanced him, Hunt sat down to write the story of his Italian life. He had intended at first to make it only that; but as all the world was full just then of the fame of the great poet so recently dead, he decided to alter and enlarge his book into an *Account of Lord Byron and his Principal Contemporaries*. And as this universal grief and praise jarred a little on his own memories, he could not resist the temptation to give the world a picture of Lord Byron as he had known him. It was the worst mistake he ever made. In the preface to the first edition he confesses — or professes — that his first inclination on finishing the book was to put it in the fire; it would have been better for him had he followed that inclination. Not that the book is not true enough. Doubtless most of the things said in it about Byron are entirely true, — there were meannesses enough in Byron ; but it was not necessary to say them, and it was peculiarly unbecoming in Hunt to say them. For, however ungracious his temper may have been, Byron had certainly laid Hunt under very material obligation. By Hunt's own confession he had paid Hunt's passage to Italy, he had lodged him in his own palace, he had paid him at one time or another three or four hundred pounds, he had relinquished to him all share in the profits of the *Liberal*. After this Hunt should certainly not have felt at liberty to write a book full of petty chatter and scandal — that Byron dreaded getting fat, that Byron couldn't bear to see women eat, that Byron had no beard, and some women liked him better for it and some didn't like him so well, with infinitude of rubbish of that sort. And if Byron in his moments of vexation had said some nasty things to Hunt, Hunt now contrived to say some very nasty things in reply. To charge Byron with licentiousness was only to echo the charge of the world; but to say that Byron was stingily careful that his pleasures should not cost him too much, — that "no Englishman ever contrived to practise more rakery and more economy at one and the same time," — this was ingeniously cruel. And for Mr. Leigh Hunt to say that Lord Byron never liked to pay a debt, — that was effrontery rising to the sublime. No man is a hero to his valet; but if the valet attempt to write the life of the hero, we know it is not the hero whose reputation is likely to suffer. It should be said to the credit of Hunt, however, that although he was at first very angry at the contemptuous criticism the book received and talked back badly in the preface to the second edition, he did afterward come to see his error and acknowledged it very handsomely in the *Autobiography*, twenty years later.

The rest of his story may be passed over more briefly. He had yet thirty years of life, but after the publication of the *Byron* in 1828, he settled down to the work of magazinist and reviewer. In the next twenty-five years he set up several other periodicals, — eight of them, — for which he furnished most or all of the copy. His various books issued from time to time, *The Seer*, *The Town*, *Table Talk*, *Men*, *Women*, *and Books*, were made up of essays selected from these and his earlier journals. Although we think of him as an easy-going dilettante, he must sometimes have toiled terribly. For example, from September 4, 1830, to February 13, 1832, he ran a daily paper, and wrote it all himself. To be sure, it was of four pages only; but if any one will propose to himself the task of writing four small folio pages of print six days in a week, for a year and a half, he will not be surprised that the work, as Hunt says, "nearly killed me." But after about this time the sky began to brighten. He did not meddle with politics any longer; but after the Reform measures of 1832, politics seemed to be coming his way, and a good many younger men remembered his services to liberalism in the days when liberalism had been very unpopular. Even his old enemies softened to him. *Blackwood's*, the worst of them all, invited him to become a contributor and made amends for the hard words of fifteen years before in Wilson's famous sentence: "The animosities are mortal, but the humanities live forever." His own temper became more mellowed, his judgments broader and more urbane. The best of his old friends were gone, Shelley,

Keats, Hazlitt, Lamb; but after about 1835 he enjoyed the acquaintance of a new generation of journalists and men of letters who all had a generous feeling for him and didn't take him too seriously. His best friends in this group were Macaulay, John Forster, and Carlyle. It is a little strange that the rugged sage of Chelsea, who had no patience with the æsthetic type and regarded such a man as Keats "a chosen vessel of hell," should have taken so kindly to his shiftless neighbor in the next street. Yet in spite of his contempt for Hunt's hugger-mugger housekeeping, it is evident that his rigor did thaw up before this vivacious little man, "chatting idly melodious as bird on bough," who came in every other night to hear Mrs. Carlyle sing old Scotch songs and share the evening oatmeal. "A man of genius," says Carlyle, "in a very strict sense of that word . . . of graceful fertility, of clearness, lovingness, truthfulness, of childlike open character." And, in turn, better or truer thing was never said of the real Thomas Carlyle than Leigh Hunt said: "I believe that what Mr. Carlyle loves better than his fault-finding with all its eloquence is the face of any human creature that looks suffering and loving and sincere." And though it has been both affirmed and denied, I have little doubt that Jane Welsh Carlyle is the Jenny of that most dainty and remembrable bit of verse Hunt ever wrote, —

"Jenny kissed me when we met,
　　Jumping from the chair she sat in;
Time, you thief who love to get
　　Sweets into your list, put that in:
Say I'm weary, say I'm sad,
　　Say that health and wealth have miss'd me,
Say I'm growing old, but add,
　　Jenny kiss'd me!"

The last ten years of his life were passed in comparative ease. It is true he never gained any mastery of the economies of life; but an annuity of a hundred and twenty pounds from the Shelley family and a pension of two hundred pounds from the Civil List made that mastery needless. His bland optimism grew on him in his declining years, and he diffused a mild glow of universal benevolence and hopefulness. He had made up all his old quarrels, forgotten all his old resentments. The one ungenerous reference to him in those years, the too faithful portrait of Harold Skimpole in Dickens' *Bleak House*, it is said he alone of all readers did not recognize until it was pointed out to him. His fame, though far more lowly than the dreams of his youth had promised, was assured. Everybody knew him, and everybody liked him. There was hardly an artist or man of letters among his contemporaries who had not some kindly word for the sprightly, bright-eyed old poet and critic who, in this present evil world, never lost his cheerful assurance

that all things are turning out best for everybody. He died August 28, 1839, at the age of
seventy-five.

II

After the lapse of half a century the man still
keeps a pleasant place in our memory. He advocated good causes always, with however much un-
wisdom; he always thought well of human nature,
— too well, — and his easy, nonchalant cheerfulness
has doubtless contributed something to the gladness
of the world. On the other hand, it must be admitted that it is impossible to have the highest
respect either for his opinions or his temper. The
great man cannot take life so easily as Leigh Hunt
always took it. Optimism like his means that the
optimist cannot or will not see life as it is, and feel
all the weight of this unintelligible world. Hunt
says that once or twice in his career he was troubled
with hypochondria, which took the form of despon-
dent wrestling with insoluble moral problems, the
origin of evil being a nightmare that gave him
especial agony. But he soon decided that the
trouble was due to his liver; in his normal moods
he was quite indifferent to such disquieting questions.
The fundamental defect in Hunt's moral nature,
I take it, was an almost entire lack of the sense of
justice, in the relations of men to each other and to a

Higher Power.   It was a matter of familiar comment among his friends that he could not distinguish between a loan and a gift, and never thought of repaying either one.   A promissory note was an everlasting mystery to him.   He says in the *Life of Byron:* "I have some peculiar notions on the subject of money . . . which will be found to involve considerable differences of opinion with the community. . . .   Among other things in which I differ in point of theory I have not that horror of being under obligation which is thought an essential refinement in money matters."   Though he adds, with unconscious humor, that in practice he has often been obliged to conform to the usage of society. But he seemed to have just as little conception of obligation of every other sort.   For lack of it, his ethics were a muddle of mawkish sentiment and lukewarm benevolence.   He himself professed, in his own words, "to partake of none of the ordinary notions of merit and demerit with regard to any one," and thought himself "neither a bit better or worse than any other man."   He who thinks so, or pretends to think so, disqualifies himself at once for any moral criticism or any just view of the great facts of human life.   A theologian would say he had no sense of sin — and the theologian would be right. He had, instead of that, a dread and hatred of all pain, by whomsoever inflicted and for whatsoever

reason. He disliked good old Izaak Walton because he found cruel pleasure in catching little
fishes; and he disliked the Jehovah of the Old
Testament because He threatens to punish thieves,
and murderers, and adulterers, and that sort of
folk. To punishment he was mildly but firmly
opposed; it was a form of payment. Dante, though
a great poet, he conceived to be "one of the most
childishly mistaken men that ever lived, a bigoted
and exasperated man," and he chastises what he
calls the "infernal opinions" of the great Italian
with much ardor. He was often concerned over
the intemperate earnestness of good people, and in
his earlier years wrote for the *Examiner* a series of
papers on *The Folly and Danger of Methodism*
that are rather amusing. Later in life, he prepared
a little pocket volume — which John Forster got
printed for him — containing his own creed and
ritual, and entitled, *Christianism, Belief and Un-
belief Reconciled*. The title may perhaps remind
us of Carlyle's scornful proposal for a Heaven and
Hell Amalgamation Society; but Hunt's method
of reconciliation is very simple — you have only to
believe what you like and disbelieve everything else,
and the thing is done. All which, of course, only
proves that Hunt had no conception how infinitely
serious a thing is this human life of ours, and how
perplexed and difficult, in the face of all its mystery,

is any deep belief at all. He shared his friend Shelley's refusal of all law and penalty, and Shelley's confidence in the power of benevolent impulse; but he never felt Shelley's pathetic despair, or Shelley's tragic conviction that the world is out of joint.

It was this very shallowness, both of opinion and feeling, joined with a certain bland assurance of manner, that made him often a difficult opponent in controversy. His critics charged him, and with some justice, of inability to understand the complexity of the questions he decided so jauntily, of a flippancy in the treatment of great passions that often passed into vulgarity, of a lack of reverence before great truths that often amounted to something like blasphemy. Yet he always took himself very seriously, and was sure, if possible, to assume the attitude of amiable but injured virtue. "If I have any two good qualities," he says complacently, "to set off against my defects, it is that I am not vindictive, and that I speak the truth." I think he did mean to speak the truth, as far as he saw it, and he was not vindictive; but he had a habit of mind far more irritating than vindictiveness — the habit of cheerful endurance of wrongs purely imaginary. The most utterly exasperating thing a man can do is to meekly forgive you for an injury you never committed; and this treatment Hunt sometimes accorded to his critics as well as to those people who were guilty of supposing he would pay the money he owed.

The charge the enemies of Hunt used to make oftenest was that both in his life and in his writings he was an under-bred, vulgar person. "I wish," said Napier, "that Hunt would write a *gentlemanly* article for the *Edinburgh.*" That was a charge likely to be made against anybody of pronounced democratic notions in the England of the early nineteenth century; and as made against Hunt, it was never exactly just. Yet Hunt's character always did lack distinction. There was nothing robust or severe about him. He was a great deal of a sentimentalist. He notes that the first words he heard in Italy were "fiore" and "donne" — flowers and ladies. In Florence he congratulated himself that he was lodged in the Via Belle Donne, till he found it was very nasty and very noisy. The one English prose-writer he admired most was Sterne; my uncle Toby he pronounced the ideal Christian, and Sterne himself the wisest man since Shakespeare. Any man who could say that must himself be something less than a gentleman. The truth is, sentimentalism is always vulgar. No man can live so largely among the mere prettinesses of life, indifferent to its noblest joys and noblest pains, without losing something of that power of vigorous and manly judgment upon which good taste — I had almost said good morals — depends.

III

If the critic is charged with paying too much attention to Hunt the man, he may reply there is no better way of understanding Hunt the writer. For all his literary work shows the same charm and the same limitations that we have found in his character. As to his poetry, there is no need to say much. He was unable to portray or to appreciate genuine passion; he had little sympathy with the more strenuous forms of action and suffering. All the higher reaches of poetry were, therefore, inaccessible to him. That is the cause of his failure in the most ambitious of his poems, *The Story of Rimini.* To retell that story of Paolo and Francesca, told once for all with the simplicity and reticence of extremest pathos, is a daring venture for any poet; but for Leigh Hunt to attempt it was the sheerest folly. He tried to give to that most poignant of tragedies a certain gentle tenderness and grace; the results, at the supreme points of the narrative, are nothing less than astounding. For example, Hunt's version of that scene where together the lovers read of Lancelot begins thus : —

> "So sat she fixed; and so observed was she
> Of one who at the door stood tenderly,

> Paulo, — who from a window seeing her
> Go straight across the lawn, and guessing where,
> Had thought she was in tears, and found, that day,
> His usual efforts vain to keep away.
> 'May I come in?' said he: — it made her start —
> That smiling voice; she colored, pressed her heart
> A moment, as for breath, and then with free
> And usual tone said, 'O yes, certainly.'"

How any human being could first read his *Dante* and then write such lines as these, is more than I can comprehend. It is one of the most incredible lapses into pure banality in English verse. And there are other passages almost as bad. Wherever the feeling should be intense and concentrated, he dilutes it into sentimental commonplace. As Laertes says in the play —

> "Thought and affliction, passion, hell itself,
> He turns to favor and to prettiness."

The only parts of the poem, therefore, that have any merits are the unessential parts, descriptive and decorative — gardens and processions, and that sort of thing. The critics professed to be scandalized by the immorality of the poem; which was absurd, especially so in a public that could accept with only mild and half-admiring expostulation Byron's worst verses. Indeed, Hunt had changed the story a little so that, as he said, he might teach a useful lesson as to the fatal results, not of passion in the lovers, but of deceit in the elder brother. The poem is moral enough; but it does show instances of a curious sort of offence against good taste found too often in all Hunt's writing, prose as well as verse. Like Sterne, whom he admired so much, he had a kind of indelicate delicacy, an affectation of innocence, that often passed into mawkishness and sometimes into pruriency.

The most important thing, however, to be said about the *Story of Rimini* is that it was the first considerable attempt in the nineteenth century to revive the rhyming ten-syllable couplet in an essentially new form. The lines are run on, the pauses are varied, the rigidity of the couplet is entirely broken up. Hunt said that he owed the suggestion of the verse to Dryden; it is obvious, too, that he was influenced by Chaucer, whose fluency and naïveté he tried to reproduce. In the preface to the collected edition of his poems, issued in 1832, he remarks: "It seems to me that, beautiful as are the compositions which the English language possesses in the heroic couplet, both by deceased and living writers, it remains for some poet hereafter to perfect the versification by making a just compromise between the inharmonious freedom of our old poets in general and the regularity of Dryden; who, noble as his management of it is, beats after all too much upon the rhyme." This was what Hunt attempted

238

to do. His attempt was not very successful; it was impossible it should be with a story of intense passion like the *Rimini*. But he must be given the credit of being the first to see and state the possibilities of this essentially new metrical form. Keats, who unquestionably learned it from Hunt, used it immediately in all his early verses, and with signal success, a little later, in the *Lamia;* and several more recent poets — notably William Morris —have proved how well it is adapted to easy, deliberate, highly decorated narrative poetry.

Some of Hunt's other and less pretentious narrative poems, like the *Hero and Leander*, are better than the *Rimini;* but in them all he is at his best when passion and action are at a mimimum, and he can find opportunity for the play of a leisurely fancy. Among English poets his favorite was Spenser, in whose land of dreams there is no passion and no real action. Throughout his work there are passages of genuinely beautiful description, and occasionally — not often — single lines of startling beauty of image. But, on the other hand, he had a weakness for sentimental and affected epithet, —which he very unfortunately imparted to Keats, — and his taste is never quite firm and sure. From his temperament and surroundings one might have expected him to write more verse like the charming rondeau quoted just now, *Jenny Kissed Me*, short occasional lyrics of love, or compliment, or playful satire. But he did not. His muse was too garrulous and gossiping for that. His satire lacks point; his humor lacks sparkle; his line lacks finish. Only three of his shorter poems are now really alive, and in each of these some serious feeling gives sincerity and restraint to the phrase: the *Abou ben Adhem*, his one familiar poem; the sonnet on the Nile, his one noble poem; and the *Lines to T. L. H.*, *Six Years Old, during a Sickness*, beginning

> "Sleep breathes at last from out thee,
> My little patient boy."

This last poem is the best example of the characteristic gentleness of Hunt, for once expressing itself without any false note. It is enough to prove that there was a genuine, if slender, vein of poetry in the man. Of course T. L. H. is his son Thornton.

For Hunt as critic, there is much more to be said. He had the first qualification of the critic, he was a lover of books. Human life interested him chiefly as stuff to be made up into literature. That was one reason why he could not be a poet — he did not like life at first hand. With reference to nature, also, he had much the same feeling. It was Charles James Fox, I believe, who once said, "There is only one thing in life more pleasant than to lie under an apple tree in June with a book; and that is to lie under an apple tree in June without a book." Hunt would always have wished the book. Indeed he seemed to care for only so much of nature as might serve for pleasant setting for his reading; he had no use for the solitudes and solemnities. No doubt this liking to look at all things through the spectacles of books may have deprived him of that freshness of view which comes from bringing everything to the test of life; but, at all events, it gave to his criticism the zest of eager personal interest. He is in love with his theme. He smacks his lips over some delicious passage of verse as if taste were to him literally a delight of sense. And he has in rather unusual degree the gift to impart this delight to the reader. Some paragraphs of his on Spenser, for example, are among the best things ever said of Spenser.

His criticism is doubtless rambling and discursive. He selects favorite passages and flits from flower to flower. His appreciation, moreover, was limited. He liked beauty, grace, luxuriance, repose; strenuous action, passion, anything rugged or sublime disconcerted him. In style he was inclined to prefer the ornate to the chaste, captivating beauty of form rather than a more severe or interior charm. Naturally, therefore, he was a better critic of manner than of matter, of poetry than of prose. Furthermore, as he had no constructive ability himself, so he had little sense of it in others. He takes his literature piecemeal, and does not appreciate the larger, more structural virtues of a great work of literary art. Similarly, he is not always able to perceive rightly the essential, distinguishing qualities of an author's genius, or to see how the particular excellences he points out so well are related to the author's personality. For example, he says of the poet he ought to have known best, Shelley, that if he had lived, he would have been the greatest dramatist since Shakespeare. This is about as mistaken a verdict as could possibly be pronounced on a genius so thoroughly self-involved and lyrical as Shelley's. But on the same page, speaking of Shelley's style, Hunt says: "Nobody has a style so orphic and primeval. His page is full of mountains, seas, and skies, of light and darkness and the seasons and all the elements of our being, as if Nature herself had written it." Such a statement, though somewhat over-rhetorical, certainly is admirably suggestive of Shelley's manner; but Hunt should have seen that this "orphic and primeval" style could never belong to a dramatist; it is the style of the lyrist, whose soul seems to lie open to every breath of inspiration "that under heaven is blown." So Hunt says of Keats that, had he lived, "he would doubtless have written in the vein of Hyperion," rising superior to the "languishments of love" that made the *Eve of St. Agnes* so over-rich and languorous. But Hunt, who knew the whole course of Keats' life, from its beginning to its end, ought to have remembered that all his latest work, the *Lamia*, the *Eve of St. Mark*, the *La Belle Dame sans Merci*, showed no tendency to the development of a classic and chastened imagination, but rather a preference for the rich and melancholy studies of mediævalism. His genius, thoroughly romantic, would in all probability, like that of Rossetti, have grown more and more in love with the mystic half-lights of the middle age.

But Hunt's detached critical remarks are almost always incisive and illuminating. Thus he says of Milton, "He had not that faith in things that Homer and Dante had, apart from the intervention of words;" that is excellent as a suggestion of the mode of Milton's imagination when compared with that of the two other great epic poets. He works himself into a rage over the doctrines of Dante's poem, declaring it (in a theological point of view) no better than the dream of a hypochondriac savage; yet he was acutely sensitive to the dramatic power of Dante, and you will look far to find a better expression of the wonderful sense of reality above the actual, the dream vividness of Dante, than Hunt gives in these few words: —

"Whatever he paints he throws, as it were, upon its own powers; as though an artist should draw figures that started into life and proceeded to action for themselves, frightening their creator. Every action, word, and look of these creatures becomes full of sensibility and suggestion. The invisible is at the back of the visible; darkness becomes palpable; silence describes a character, nay, forms the most striking part of a story; a word acts as a flash of lightning, which displays some gloomy neighborhood, where a tower is standing with dreadful faces at the windows; or where at your feet, full of eternal voices, one abyss is beheld dropping out of another in the lurid light of torment. . . . Dante has the minute probabilities of a Defoe in the midst of the loftiest poetry."

Hunt's critical writing, however, is not all desultory and empirical. His contributions to literary theory are by no means insignificant. He had considerable power of analysis and definition, and he had thought more carefully upon the grounds of literary excellence than upon any other subject. He took especial interest in the essential nature and the technique of poetry. The preface to the volume of 1832, from which I just now quoted his statement as to the modification of the heroic couplet, contains an admirable discussion of the essentials of poetic matter and form; while his fuller treatment of the subject, ten years later, in the essay entitled *What is Poetry?* is, on the whole, as satisfactory an answer

to that difficult question as any more recent writer
has been able to give us. To be sure, Hunt does not
delve very deeply in his subject, and he is afraid of an
exhaustive treatment — for which we may be thank-
ful; but the essay is full of the most acute and discriminating remark. His discussion of the value
of musical sensibility in verse, of the difference
between smoothness and sweetness, of the effect of
variety in accent, of alliteration and assonance, his
distinction between the natural and the prosaic, —
which very neatly punctures the fallacy in Wordsworth's famous preface, — these, among other passages, may be cited in proof of the delicacy and justice of his taste when dealing with general principles.
The whole paper is very suggestive; and it is very
entertaining. It serves as an introduction to the
volume he called *Imagination and Fancy*, the rest
of the book being made up of a body of selections
from our poetry illustrating the principles of the essay
with a running comment. It was natural for Hunt
to consider the imagination as the faculty that em-
bellishes and interprets, rather than in its higher
creative functions; indeed, it was almost inevitable
he should do so, if he was to exhibit it in brief selections. He is, therefore, led to lay perhaps undue
stress upon the imagery and music of poetry as compared with its higher values of thought and feeling.
Yet, on the whole, I do not know any volume better

fitted to guide and stimulate a growing taste; there is hardly anything better to put into the hands of a young student of poetry. A companion volume, made up in the same way, illustrating wit and humor, is almost as good. Both books were written after Hunt was sixty years old; it is to be regretted that he did not live to carry out his purpose of adding to these volumes three more, treating respectively of action and passion, of contemplation, and of song. For his taste grew steadily broader and sounder, and in his later years he lived to appreciate very justly authors — Wordsworth and Scott, for example — that in his youth he had sadly misjudged.

But far the greater part of Hunt's work was in the form of the short periodical essay. He had fallen in love, as we have seen, with the eighteenth-century essayists while in his early teens; and his first purely literary venture, — if we except the juvenile poems, — the *Reflector*, issued in 1810, was modelled closely upon Addison and Goldsmith. Here, again, I think Hunt may be credited with rejuvenating an old literary form. For the *Reflector* was the first really successful attempt in the nineteenth century to revive the light periodical essay, after its ponderous mishandling by Johnson in the *Rambler* and *Idler*. We shall remember that Hunt's work of this kind preceded that of Lamb and Hazlitt; indeed it was in periodicals set up by Hunt that both Lamb and Hazlitt found a medium for the publication of some of their best work. When, a little later, the magazines began to appear, there was a demand for this sort of writing — as there has been ever since. We, perhaps, in the twentieth century, think ourselves a little too earnest for this kind of literature; yet if any man can write it as well, for example, as Thackeray wrote it in his *Roundabout Papers*, he will be sure of readers to-day, if not of fame to-morrow. But no kind of writing above mere journalism is more ephemeral. Not only the *Rambler* and the *Idler*, but the *Bee* and the *Citizen of the World*, and even the *Tatler* and the *Spectator*, it is to be feared, now repose undisturbed upon the top shelves; and Hunt's *Indicators* and *Companions* have doubtless joined them there. It is only some remarkable dexterity of style or some unique humor or force of personality that can keep such work from oblivion. Hunt had neither of these qualifications. His gossiping papers are very pleasant reading, if you have time on your hands; but they have no compelling charm. After all we have been told of the fascinating converse of the man, we are surprised to find his wit has so little keenness, and his humor is only often a playful, half-patronizing familiarity. Then, again, he is a little too bookish. More than half his papers are nothing but echoes of his reading — old stories retold, bits of legend or romance, scraps from his favorite authors. And even those drawn directly from the life of the street or the fields seem to lack that humorous observation of men and things at first hand that makes the papers of Steele, for example, so racy. If Hunt is writing on coaches, or May-day or London fog, he is sure to tell you what the poets and historians think about it, and may give you a score of quotations in three pages. Nor has Hunt the power to show by some sudden flash of imagination the subtle connection of the simplest things with the most serious, as Lamb can do, or to pass almost insensibly on any familiar occasion into a train of lofty and solemn revery, as Hazlitt so frequently does. A comparison of his work in this respect with Hazlitt's will show how inferior is Hunt's. He never has Hazlitt's marvellous acuteness of analysis; he never has Hazlitt's serious, half-mournful, but large and inspiring tone of reflection, Hazlitt's imagination and passion, Hazlitt's rhythm and distinction of manner.

Yet, after all, it is ungenerous to find fault with a man for not doing better what he has done so well. For, leaving out his second-hand stories, and admitting that his humor is often insipid and his sentiment wilted, we could still select from Hunt's writing a goodly volume of essays hard to surpass in their kind. They are made up of trifles; but then life is made up of trifles. We need not withhold some cordial liking from that kind of literature which does not attempt to arouse or inspire, but rather to express the familiar pleasures that cheer, and the familiar trials that chasten, the hours of every day. Hunt doesn't show us new things, or even new meanings in the old things. He talks with us as we talk with each other around the fire on winter evenings, of our habits, our likings, our prejudices, our tasks, our books, our clothes; about taxes or the weather; about the last play we have seen or the last pretty girl we have met, — for Hunt at sixty, with nine children, was still a youngster, — or, as the evening wears and our mood grows a shade more serious, about our comforts, our plans, our fancies, our friends, and — for Hunt was always more a benedict than a bachelor — about all the snug domesticities of home. He makes no exactions upon your thought, and he seldom invades your emotions beyond that outer circle friends may approach but may not cross. Such papers do not rank very high as literature. One has a comfortable feeling that he can leave them alone, if he likes, without endangering his reputation as a well-read man. Yet you may turn over the pages of our best magazines of to-day without finding much editorial writing that, for interest, might not well be exchanged for these little papers of Leigh Hunt.

His name not unfitly closes the short list of writers considered in this volume. His career was longer than that of any other, for his first book appeared in

1801 and his last in 1855. Perhaps in this long life he had neither done nor suffered quite so much as he himself, when near its close, was inclined to believe. He was not of the stuff that scorns delights and lives laborious days. He had solved no problems, inspired no heroisms, written no masterpieces. But he did something in early life for the cause of civil liberty; he did more, I think, in his later years to quicken and widen the love of good literature. And through all that half-century, by three generations of friends, he was known as a genial, cheery man, who never felt the tedium of life, was hopeful under all its discouragements, impatient of all harshness, fond of all gentle and beautiful things. Doubtless he was too self-indulgent to be the ideal philanthropist; yet we may, with no fulsome exaggeration, accord to him the praise he himself would most have coveted, phrased in his own best words: —

"Write me as one who loved his fellow-men."